TECHNICAL
REPORT

T0302504

Analysis of Racial Disparities in the New York Police Department's Stop, Question, and Frisk Practices

Greg Ridgeway

Sponsored by the New York City Police Foundation

RAND Safety and Justice

A RAND INFRASTRUCTURE, SAFETY, AND ENVIRONMENT PROGRAM

The research described in this report was supported by the New York City Police Foundation and was conducted under the auspices of the Center on Quality Policing (CQP), part of the Safety and Justice Program within RAND Infrastructure, Safety, and Environment (ISE).

Library of Congress Cataloging-in-Publication Data is available for this publication.

ISBN 978-0-8330-4515-7

Published 2007 by the RAND Corporation
1776 Main Street, P.O. Box 2138, Santa Monica, CA 90407-2138
1200 South Hayes Street, Arlington, VA 22202-5050
4570 Fifth Avenue, Suite 600, Pittsburgh, PA 15213-2665
RAND URL: http://www.rand.org/
To order RAND documents or to obtain additional information, contact
Distribution Services: Telephone: (310) 451-7002;
Fax: (310) 451-6915; Email: order@rand.org

Preface

In February 2007, the New York City Police Department (NYPD) released statistics that indicated that more than a half-million pedestrians had been stopped on suspicion of a crime in New York City in 2006. Almost 90 percent of the stops involved nonwhites. The department immediately faced questions regarding its stop, question, and frisk (SQF) patterns and practices. The department contacted the RAND Center on Quality Policing (CQP) to conduct an objective analysis of data collected in street encounters between the police and the public, and the New York City Police Foundation funded a project that began later that month.

This report documents the methods and findings from the RAND researchers' analysis of NYPD's SQF data. This report should be of interest to NYPD executives and command staff and New York City policymakers and community members. This report may also prove useful to residents and officials in other jurisdictions where similar practices are under consideration and similar issues are being confronted. Related RAND work that may be of interest to readers of this report includes the following:

- *Police-Community Relations in Cincinnati* (Riley et al., 2005)
- *Police-Community Relations in Cincinnati: Year Two Evaluation Report* (Ridgeway et al., 2006)
- *Testing for Racial Profiling in Traffic Stops From Behind a Veil of Darkness* (Grogger and Ridgeway, 2006)
- *Assessing the Effect of Race Bias in Post-Traffic Stop Outcomes Using Propensity Scores* (Ridgeway, 2006)
- *Race and the Decision to Seek the Death Penalty in Federal Cases* (Klein, Berk, and Hickman, 2006)
- *Police Personnel Challenges After September 11: Anticipating Expanded Duties and a Changing Labor Pool* (Raymond et al., 2005)
- *Assessing Racial Profiling More Credibly* (Ridgeway and Riley, 2004).

The RAND Center on Quality Policing

This research was conducted under the auspices of the Center on Quality Policing (CQP), part of the Safety and Justice Program within RAND Infrastructure, Safety, and Environment (ISE). The center's mission is to help guide the efforts of police agencies to improve the efficiency, effectiveness, and fairness of their operations. The center's research and analysis focus on force planning (e.g., recruitment, retention, training), performance measurement, cost-effective best practices, and use of technology, as well as issues in police-community relations. The mission of RAND Infrastructure, Safety, and Environment is to improve the development, operation, use, and protection of society's essential physical assets and natural resources and to enhance the related social assets of safety and security of individuals in transit and in their workplaces and communities. Safety and Justice Program research addresses occupational safety, transportation safety, food safety, and public safety including violence, policing, corrections, substance abuse, and public integrity.

Questions or comments about this report should be sent to the project leader, Greg Ridgeway (Greg_Ridgeway@rand.org). Information is available online about the Safety and Justice Program (http://www.rand.org/ise/safety) and the CQP (http://www.rand.org/ise/centers/quality_policing/). Inquiries about the CQP should be made to its associate director, Jeremy Wilson (Jeremy_Wilson@rand.org). Inquiries about research projects should be sent to the following address:

Greg Ridgeway, Acting Director
Safety and Justice Program, ISE
RAND Corporation
1776 Main Street
P.O. Box 2138
Santa Monica, CA 90407-2138
310-393-0411, x7734
Greg_Ridgeway@rand.org

Contents

Figures

Tables

Summary

In 2006, the New York City Police Department (NYPD) was involved in a half-million encounters with pedestrians who were stopped because of suspected criminal involvement. Raw statistics for these encounters suggest large racial disparities—89 percent of the stops involved nonwhites. Fifty-three percent of the stops involved black suspects, 29 percent Hispanic, 11 percent white, and 3 percent Asian, and race was unknown for the remaining 4 percent of the stops. Forty-five percent of black and Hispanic suspects were frisked, compared with 29 percent of white suspects; yet, when frisked, white suspects were 70 percent likelier than black suspects to have had a weapon on them.

These figures raise critical questions: first, whether they point to racial bias in police officers' decisions to stop particular pedestrians, and, further, whether they indicate that officers are particularly intrusive when stopping nonwhites.

Seeking answers, the NYPD turned to RAND to help it gain a clearer understanding of this issue and identify recommendations for addressing potential problems identified in the analysis. To examine the issue, RAND researchers analyzed data on all street encounters between NYPD officers and pedestrians in 2006, more than 500,000 stops that officers documented in SQF report worksheets (NYPD Unified Form 250 or UF250; see Appendix D for a reproduction).

RAND researchers conducted three types of analysis. First, we compared the racial distribution of stops to a variety of benchmarks. This process, commonly referred to as *external benchmarking*, attempts to construct what the racial distribution of the stopped pedestrians would have been if officers' stop decisions had been racially unbiased. Constructing valid external benchmarks is a difficult task, since it involves assessing the racial composition of those participating in criminal activity and the racial composition of those exposed to the patrolling officers. Both the rates of criminal participation and police exposure are challenging to estimate. We completed analyses using several candidate benchmarks, each of which has strengths and weaknesses for providing plausible external benchmarks. For example, residential census data—that is, the racial distribution of the general population in New York—possibly provide an estimate of the racial distribution of those exposed to police but do not reflect rates of criminal participation. As a result, external benchmarks based on the census have been widely discredited. The racial distribution of arrestees has been proposed as a more reliable benchmark. A more promising external benchmark is the racial distribution of individuals identified in crime-suspect descriptions, though this benchmark also has serious pitfalls.

Second, we compared each individual officer's stopping patterns with a benchmark constructed from stops in similar circumstances made by other officers. This process, known as *internal benchmarking*, avoids the primary limitations of external benchmarking and is useful for flagging officers who are substantially overstopping nonwhites compared to their peers.

Third, we examined the outcomes of stops, assessing whether stopped white and nonwhite suspects have different rates of frisks, searches, uses of force, and arrests.

The results from these three analyses are described in more detail in the chapters that follow.

It is worth noting that most of the report focuses on comparisons between stops involving black, Hispanic, and white suspects. Concerns of racial bias also pertain to other racial groups and ethnic subgroups, such as those from Asia. Asians represent 3 percent of all stops, a relatively small proportion. However, and unfortunately, statistical analysis is unreliable under those circumstances.

Results of External-Benchmarking Analysis

Evaluating racial disparities in pedestrian stops using external benchmarks is highly sensitive to the choice of benchmark. Therefore, analyses based on any of the external benchmarks developed to date are questionable.

Benchmarks based on crime-suspect descriptions may provide a good measure of the rates of participation in certain types of crimes by race, but being a valid benchmark requires that suspects, regardless of race, are equally exposed to police officers.

We found that black pedestrians were stopped at a rate that is 20 to 30 percent lower than their representation in crime-suspect descriptions. Hispanic pedestrians were stopped disproportionately more, by 5 to 10 percent, than their representation among crime-suspect descriptions would predict.

We provide comparisons with several other benchmarks to demonstrate the sensitivity of external benchmarking. The arrest benchmark has been featured prominently in previous analyses of NYPD stop patterns (Spitzer, 1999; Gelman, Fagan, and Kiss, 2007). However, arrests may not accurately reflect the types of suspicious activity that officers might observe, arrests can occur far from where the crime occurred, and, since police make both the arrests and the stops, the arrest benchmark is not independent of any biases that officers might have.

Black pedestrians were stopped at nearly the same rate as their representation among arrestees would suggest. Hispanic suspects appear to be stopped at a rate slightly higher (6 percent higher) than their representation among arrestees.

The most widely used, but least reliable, benchmark is the residential census. Census benchmarks do not account for differential rates of crime participation by race or for differential exposure to the police. Comparisons to the residential census are not suitable for assessing racial bias.

Black pedestrians were stopped at a rate that is 50 percent greater than their representation in the residential census. The stop rate for Hispanic pedestrians equaled their residential-census representation.

Results of Internal-Benchmarking Analysis

This analysis compared the racial distribution of each officer's stops to a benchmark racial distribution constructed to match the officer's stops on time, place, and several other stop features.

This analysis found the following:

- Five officers appear to have stopped substantially more black suspects than other officers did when patrolling the same areas, at the same times, and with the same assignment. Nine officers stopped substantially fewer black suspects than expected.
- Ten officers appear to have stopped substantially more Hispanic suspects than other officers did when patrolling the same areas, at the same times, and with the same assignment. Four officers stopped substantially fewer Hispanic suspects than expected.
- Six of the 15 flagged officers are from the Queens South borough.

To put these findings into perspective, the analysis flagged 0.5 percent of the 2,756 NYPD officers most active in pedestrian-stop activity. Those 2,756 most active officers, about 7 percent of the total number of officers, accounted for 54 percent of the total number of 2006 stops. The remaining stops were made by another 15,855 officers, for whom an accurate internal benchmark could not be constructed, mostly because they conducted too few stops. While the data suggest that only a small fraction of the officers most active in pedestrian stops may be outliers, the stops made by the 15,855 that we could not analyze may still be of concern.

Results of Outcome Analysis

If there is race bias in the behavior of the 15,000-plus officers whose individual behavior we could not analyze with the internal benchmark, it may still reveal itself in the patterns of stop outcomes—that is, post-stop frisks, searches, uses of force, and arrests. Therefore we analyzed the outcomes of police stops.

Our analysis found the following:

- Officers frisked white suspects slightly less frequently than they did *similarly situated* nonwhites (29 percent of stops versus 33 percent of stops). Black suspects are slightly likelier to have been frisked than white suspects stopped in circumstances similar to the black suspects (46 percent versus 42 percent). While there is a gap, this difference is much smaller than what the aggregate statistics indicated.
- The rates of searches were nearly equal across racial groups, between 6 and 7 percent. However, in Staten Island, the rate of searching nonwhite suspects was significantly greater than that of searching white suspects.
- White suspects were slightly likelier to be issued a summons than were similarly situated nonwhite suspects (5.7 percent versus 5.2 percent). On the other hand, arrest rates for white suspects were slightly lower than those for similarly situated nonwhites (4.8 percent versus 5.1 percent).
- Officers were slightly less likely to use force against white suspects than they were to use it against similarly situated nonwhites (15 percent versus 16 percent); however, in Queens,

Brooklyn North, and the Bronx, there was no evidence that use-of-force rates varied across races.

- Officers recovered contraband (such as weapons, illegal drugs, or stolen property) in 6.4 percent of the stops of white suspects. The contraband recovery rate was 5.7 percent for similarly situated black suspects and 5.4 percent for similarly situated Hispanic suspects.

Overall, after adjustment for stop circumstances, we generally found small racial differences in the rates of frisk, search, use of force, and arrest. Nonwhites generally experienced slightly more intrusive stops, in terms of having more frequent frisks and searches, than did similarly situated white suspects. While most racial differences in post-stop outcomes were small, for some outcomes in some boroughs, the gaps warrant a closer review. For example, the Staten Island borough stands out particularly with several large racial gaps in the frisk rates (20 percent of whites versus 29 percent of similarly situated blacks), search rates (5 percent for whites versus 8 percent of similarly situated blacks), and use-of-force rates (10 percent for whites and 14 percent for similarly situated blacks).

The raw numbers on recovery rates for contraband indicated that frisked or searched white suspects were much likelier to have contraband than were black suspects. However, after accounting for several important factors, the disparity reduces sharply. The recovery rate for frisked or searched white suspects stopped in circumstances similar to those of black suspects was slightly greater than it was for black suspects (6.4 percent versus 5.7 percent). When considering only recovery rates of weapons, we found no differences by race. For every 1,000 frisks of black suspects, officers recovered seven weapons, and, for every 1,000 frisks of similarly situated white suspects, officers recovered eight weapons, a difference that is not statistically significant.

Conclusions

The raw statistics cited in the first paragraph of this summary distort the magnitude and, at times, the existence of racially biased policing. For example, we found that there are some legitimate factors that explain much of the difference between the frisk rate of black suspects (45 percent) and the frisk rate of white suspects (29 percent). Some of those factors include police policies and practices that can legitimately differ by time, place, and reason for the stop. As a result, the raw statistics, while easy to compute, often exaggerate racial disparities. Any racial disparities in the data are cause for concern. However, accurately measuring the magnitude of the problem can help police management, elected officials, and community members decide between the need for incremental changes in policy, reporting, and oversight or sweeping organizational changes.

Our results using more precise benchmarks do not eliminate the observed racial disparities. However, they do indicate that the disparities are much smaller than the raw statistics would suggest. This result does not absolve the NYPD of the need to monitor the issue, but it also implies that a large-scale restructuring of NYPD SQF policies and procedures is unwarranted.

Recommendations

Overall, we have six recommendations for NYPD to improve interactions between police and pedestrians during stops and to improve the accuracy of data collected during pedestrian stops.

Officers Should Clearly Explain to Pedestrians Why They Are Being Stopped

In 90 percent of the stops, the detained individual is neither arrested nor issued a summons. To mitigate the discomfort of such interactions and to bolster community trust, officers should explain the reason for the stop, discuss specifically the suspect's manner that generated the suspicion, and offer the contact information of a supervisor or appropriate complaint authority, so that the person stopped can convey any positive or negative comments about the interaction. While the latter suggestion might increase the number of official complaints, it might also reduce the number of unofficial complaints that would otherwise circulate in the suspect's social network. For a trial period in select precincts, the NYPD could require that officers give an information card to those stopped pedestrians who are neither arrested nor issued a summons. An evaluation of the program could identify the kinds of stops likeliest to result in positive or negative feedback from the stopped pedestrians. Most important, ongoing communication and negotiation with the community about SQF activities are helpful in maintaining good police-community relations.

The NYPD Should Review the Boroughs with the Largest Racial Disparities in Stop Outcomes

For most stop outcomes in most parts of the city, we found few, if any, racial differences in the rates of frisk, search, arrest, and use of force. However, for some particular subsets of stops, there are racial disparities, and, in some boroughs for some outcomes, the disparities are fairly large. In particular, there was evidence of large racial differences in frisk rates in several boroughs. For example, on Staten Island, officers frisked 20 percent of white suspects and 29 percent of similarly situated black suspects. Officers were likelier to use force of some kind against black suspects in Brooklyn South than they were to use it against similarly situated white suspects (29 percent versus 22 percent). However, the use-of-force finding on which we base this recommendation may be the result of incomplete details on the reason officers used force, the subject of the next recommendation. Regardless, a closer review of these outcomes in these boroughs may suggest changes in training, policies, or practices that can reduce these disparities.

The UF250 Should Be Revised to Capture Data on Use of Force

All of the reported differences resulting from our analysis are potentially due to unobserved or unmeasured features of the stops rather than racial bias. For example, the 1 percent difference observed in rates of use of force between stops of white and nonwhite suspects may be due to a factor not recorded on the UF250. It is possible that nonwhite suspects were slightly likelier to attempt to flee or threaten officers. If the percentage of nonwhite-pedestrian stops in which the suspect resisted officers was 0.8 percent more than the frequency with which white suspects resisted officers, then, statistically, the frisk rates would be indistinguishable. However, these reasons—attempting to flee or resisting officers—are not recorded on the UF250. The UF250 was intended for investigative purposes and not for assessing officer performance or racial disparities. For the data to be more useful for careful analysis of racial bias in use-of-force incidents, the reason for the use of force needs to be recorded.

New Officers Should Be Fully Conversant with Stop, Question, and Frisk Documentation Policies

Officers with more than one year of experience seemed fully informed of the SQF practices and documentation policies. However, informal discussions with and observations of recent academy graduates indicated that some were not fully aware of the documentation policies and procedures, despite a substantial investment of time in the academy training curriculum on SQF. This is an issue that likely impacts a small fraction of stops. For the purposes of assessing racial bias, we do not find a need for investment to correct this, but, since data on UF250s are used in other facets of NYPD evaluation, some correction in training during new officers' initial days on the street might be in order, particularly for any evaluation of Operation Impact programs.

NYPD Should Consider Modifying the Audits of the UF250

The NYPD has multiple layers of auditing to ensure that the UF250s are complete and contain valid and sufficiently detailed entries to each question. This does not address whether stops are occurring that are not documented. Since officers have an incentive to demonstrate productivity through UF250s, most stops should be documented. However, particularly problematic ones may not be. Radio communications could be monitored for a fixed period in a few randomly selected precincts. Notes of the times and places of street encounters that should have associated UF250s can be noted and requests made for the forms.

All of our analyses rely on the data that officers record on UF250s. The accuracy of the information on the forms, such as time, place, and reason for the stop, is assumed to be approximately correct for the purposes of our analyses. For inaccuracies to adversely affect our analyses, officers would have had to consistently record events differently for nonwhites than they did for white suspects. However, unless officers were carefully tabulating which actions they failed to report, the analyses in this report would interpret the patterns that would result as evidence of a disparity. For example, if officers consistently did not record frisks of nonwhite suspects, then our analysis would have found white suspects to be substantially overfrisked. There is no evidence of such general patterns. That said, in interpreting the findings of this study, we must offer the caveat that systematic misreporting of data on the UF250 could potentially distort the findings.

NYPD Should Identify, Flag, and Investigate Officers with Out-of-the-Ordinary Stop Patterns

Our analysis indicates that the racial distribution of stops for several officers is skewed substantially from those of their colleagues. We recommend that the NYPD review these flagged officers and incorporate into their early warning system a component that flags officers with extreme deviations from their colleagues. These measured disparities are evidence that these officers differ substantially from their peers; however, they are not necessarily conclusive evidence that these officers practice racially biased policing. Supervisors may then investigate and address the disparities.

Acknowledgments

I would like to thank Lorie Fridell, Paul Heaton, Jeremy Wilson, and Andrew Morral, who provided comments on drafts of this report, as well as David Adamson and Lisa Bernard who helped polish the final report. Although I benefited from these reviews, I alone remain responsible for errors and omissions in this analysis.

Abbreviations

BJS	Bureau of Justice Statistics
CPW	criminal possession of a weapon
CQP	Center on Quality Policing
fdr	false discovery rate
GLA	grand larceny, auto
ICO	integrity control officer
NYPD	New York City Police Department
OLBS	Online Booking System
SQF	stop, question, and frisk
UF250	Unified Form 250

CHAPTER ONE

Introduction: Review of the New York City Police Department's Stop, Question, and Frisk Policy and Practices

Introduction

In February 2007, the New York City Police Department (NYPD) engaged the RAND Corporation to analyze data that NYPD officers had collected on stop, question, and frisk (SQF) forms (Unified Forms 250, or UF250s) to understand whether the data from stops documented in the forms indicated racial bias. The department provided NYPD identification cards permitting RAND researchers to freely enter police headquarters, provided access to NYPD officers and staff at all ranks, and furnished data that RAND requested. On March 11, 2007, RAND researchers received and began analyzing a data set of 506,491 UF250s (see Appendix D for a copy of the UF250), documenting street encounters that occurred in 2006. In addition, the researchers studied the training curriculum associated with the UF250, met with officers responsible for training other officers in their precincts,[1] and observed officers on the streets involved in SQF street encounters.[2] This report describes the SQF policies and procedures, documents our analysis of the UF250 data, and interprets the findings of the analysis.

An endless number of queries could be put to these data. The data can be sliced in many ways: by suspected crime, by borough, by stop outcome, and so on. We have crafted this report to focus on the main questions directed at the NYPD and the main questions that stakeholders in this process are likely to ask. In particular, we address whether the racial distribution of the stops suggests racial bias, whether certain officers seem to be disproportionately stopping nonwhites, and whether there are racial differences in the rates of frisk, search, recovery of contraband, use of force, and arrest.

All of these analyses examine general patterns, averages, and rates. Any findings that do not suggest racial bias are not intended to deny any individuals' personal experiences with NYPD officers. Even though, in some comparisons, we find no differences across the racial groups on average, this obviously does not imply that individuals always have pleasant experiences with the police or even that all encounters are bias free. These analyses are helpful in understanding whether the frisk that a nonwhite pedestrian in New York might have perceived to be unnecessary is part of a pattern at NYPD of frisking nonwhites at higher rates or an incident that deserves individual attention through a complaint process rather than a department-wide change in policies and practices.

---

[1] The seven training officers interviewed were from precincts from throughout the city and were selected based on their availability to come to the police headquarters.

[2] Observations were conducted in one night shift over the course of eight hours in and around an NYPD impact area. Three hours were spent in an unmarked NYPD vehicle, one hour at the precinct, and four hours in a marked NYPD patrol car. The observed officers were either on foot patrol or assigned to a patrol car.

Levels of Police-Initiated Contacts Between Police and Citizens in New York State

In the state of New York, the courts have recognized four levels of police-initiated contacts between police and the public (*People v. De Bour*, 40 N.Y.2d 210, 1976). The rights of the citizen and the authority of the officer vary greatly across the four levels.

Level 1: Request for Information

While officers are not authorized to question any individuals at random, an officer can approach an individual for any articulable reason. The officer may ask basic questions about the individual's identity, reason for being in the area, or facts related to the reason the officer approached in the first place, such as a concern for the individual's health or safety. The citizen has no obligation to answer, cannot be subject to search, and is free to walk away.

Level 2: Common-Law Right of Inquiry

An officer may ask more probing questions when the officer believes (has "founded suspicion") that an individual may be involved in criminal activity, but the officer has no additional information to raise suspicion to the third level, described next. This officer's belief may develop as a result of a request for information if, for instance, the individual gives false answers to a request for information. The officer may ask to search the individual or the individual's bags, but, at this level, the officer cannot force the individual to answer questions, and the individual may walk away from the officer.

Level 3: Stop, Question, and Frisk

This level is reached when the officer has *reasonable suspicion* that a person is involved in criminal activity. This suspicion may result from the individual matching a crime suspect's description, carrying objects commonly used in a crime, such as a lockout tool (e.g., a slim jim), or fleeing from the scene of a recent crime. The difference between levels 2 and 3 is subtle and is the subject of many court decisions regarding proper search and seizure. The officer may frisk an individual for weapons to ensure the safety of the officer conducting the questioning. The officer may ask for identification, request an explanation for the observed suspicious behavior, and detain the individual until the officer can determine whether the individual is involved in criminal activity.

This level is the only level that should be documented on NYPD's UF250. Stops may begin as either of the first two levels and rise to the level of an SQF incident, which would be documented. An SQF incident that leads to an arrest should also produce documentation with the UF250. However, arrests that occur directly from a level-4 encounter, described next, should not be documented on a UF250.

Level 4: Arrest

When an officer has *probable cause* to believe that an individual was involved in a crime, the officer may arrest the suspect. Such situations include officers witnessing the crime, suspects being caught red-handed, or incidents in which victims identify the perpetrator. Officers should generally search the suspect for weapons or evidence, and the officers may use reasonable force to keep the suspect detained and to conduct the search.

The distinctions among these can be confusing in some instances, and this can affect which encounters officers actually document with UF250s. For example, if an officer detains a suspect who matches the description of an assailant given by the victim and then the victim positively identifies the suspect as the assailant, the officer should document this encounter on the UF250, because it began as a stop for reasonable suspicion of a crime. If, instead, the officer was with the victim and the victim pointed out the suspect across the street, the officer has probable cause to believe that the identified person has committed a crime, and no UF250 needs to be completed. Regardless of policy, however, there is a strong incentive for officers to complete the UF250 anyway, to provide further documentation of the incident and indicate the officer's productivity.

The difficulty of classifying some instances arises in discussions with officers. One Operation Impact officer,[3] a few weeks out of the academy, noted that UF250s are completed "when I stop someone that fits a criminal suspect description and it turns out not to be the person we were looking for." While that is true, the UF250 should also be completed when the suspect turns out to be the person for whom the officer was looking and is subsequently arrested. This difficulty points to the need for appropriate training.

Training of Officers on Stop, Question, and Frisk Policies

The NYPD academy trains new recruits on legal background issues during the first trimester of the academy in seven sessions lasting a total of 10.5 hours. In addition, students participate in a 4.5-hour SQF workshop. All patrol officers in the department receive regular training on SQF at their precincts during roll call. Training officers indicated that they discuss the topic of UF250s in this forum about once every two months. To assist in communicating the law and NYPD policy on the issue, the NYPD legal bureau has prepared a video series describing each of the levels of interactions. As of this writing, precinct training officers have been shown videos covering the first three levels. Last, all officers also carry in their memo books a summary sheet of these levels and instructions on what they can and cannot do during the encounters (NYPD, 2000).

We asked officers about SQF policy to determine whether the training had been retained. Officers who were fresh out of the academy seemed particularly confused about when to document stops, as the earlier quote from the Operation Impact officer indicates. We observed another Operation Impact officer stopping and frisking a pedestrian who matched a description of a boy wanted for a robbery that had occurred a few minutes earlier. An interview of the frisked pedestrian moments later suggested that the officer did not explain the reason for the stop, although the individual did not speak English well and may not have understood. A subsequent interview of the officer who conducted the stop and frisk indicated that the officer was not sure whether a UF250 should be completed. After questions about paperwork and some prodding, the officer eventually responded that such a stop should be documented in a UF250. A later check confirmed that this officer documented the stop with a UF250.

While it appears that some of the newest members of the force are uncertain about how to document street encounters properly, this is not entirely surprising. The interviewed officers

---

[3] Operation Impact places new graduates from the NYPD academy on foot posts in crime "hot spots" around New York City.

are working essentially alone in extremely busy areas and are learning to put their academy training into practice. Officers interviewed who had a year or more on the job knew the policies and the practices well and expressed no confusion on the issue.

NYPD has several layers of auditing to check that UF250s are complete and have valid entries. First, a supervisor within each command reviews completed UF250s. Second, data-entry staff screen forms for missing entries or illegible fields. Third, NYPD has a police-initiated enforcement program that each command's integrity control officer (ICO) manages. The program involves the ICO reviewing, monthly, five arrests resulting from police-initiated contact, checking that the arrests have been properly documented (including a UF250), and assessing the accuracy of the associated UF250. The Quality Assurance Division also audits the ICO's audits. Last, NYPD's Quality Assurance Division periodically selects a date and then collects from each command (each precinct, transit and housing division, crime unit, and task forces) the 25 most recent UF250s. Auditors complete a worksheet check for particularly critical elements: the suspected crime and whether it is a felony or penal-law misdemeanor, the circumstances leading up to the stop, documentation of frisks and searches, the race and sex of the suspect, and the name of the officer who made the stop. The audit in the last quarter of 2006 revealed some deficiencies. Depending on the patrol borough, in 3 to 9 percent of the stops, the race was not recorded. The cases with race missing are few enough so that it is unlikely to affect the results of the analysis. For other stop features critical to our analysis, the audits suggest that the data are fairly complete. Audited stops indicate that officers generally documented the suspected crime accurately. In the database, the suspected crime is recorded in 99.4 percent of the stops. For the remaining 0.6 percent of the stops, the suspected crimes were too vague, frequently recorded as "misdemeanor" or "felony."

While these steps might result in UF250s that are filled out completely and legibly, there is no auditing process to ensure that officers complete a UF250 for every police-initiated contact. To examine the SQF process, we spent time with patrol officers, observing their practices. In one eight-hour shift, we noted a dozen encounters that should be documented and, with a later check, confirmed that they had been.

In addition, we monitored precinct radio communications for information on other stops in the precinct. In one instance, an assault-and-robbery victim gave a description of the suspects. A pedestrian directed officers to a train platform, where officers found three men, two of whom matched the description. The officers detained the three, and the victim soon confirmed them as the assailants. Officers correctly submitted three UF250s for this interaction, since the initial contact was for reasonable suspicion of a crime. The subsequent positive identification by the victim gave the officers probable cause for the arrest.

The description of the suspects at the time was vague, giving only race and a loose description of clothes ("black jeans"). A weak description, possibly due in part to a victim's memory, increases the risk that innocent pedestrians will be detained. Radio traffic just before the arrest for the assault and robbery indicated two other street encounters of suspects. One of these encounters was with an individual about 30 years of age in a stop lasting more than 10 minutes, a rather long stop of an individual who was quite different from the actual perpetrators (a group of teenagers). Good suspect descriptions not only help solve crimes; they have the extra benefit of decreasing the risk of unnecessary negative interactions between the police and the public.

The remainder of the report focuses on the analysis of the UF250s. Chapter Two provides basic statistics from the UF250 database. In Chapter Three, we compare the racial distribution of stops to the racial distribution of the residential census, arrestees, and criminal suspects. In Chapter Four, we examine each officer's collection of stops to see whether the racial distribution of those stops differs from the racial distribution of similarly situated stops made by other officers. Lastly, in Chapter Five, we compare the outcomes of stops across race groups, assessing differences in rates of frisk, search, use of force, and arrest.

CHAPTER TWO

Description of the 2006 Stop, Question, and Frisk Data

In 2006, NYPD officers documented 506,491 stops. The stops occurred throughout the city's five boroughs, as shown in the map in Figure 2.1. The map shades the NYPD precincts by the number of stops per 1,000 people in the daytime population. Such a rate is particularly important in places like Manhattan, where the daytime population can swell by a factor of 20 or more. It does show that pedestrians in certain areas of the city have a greater chance of being stopped by police than in others.

Figure 2.1
Stops per 1,000 People (estimated daytime population)

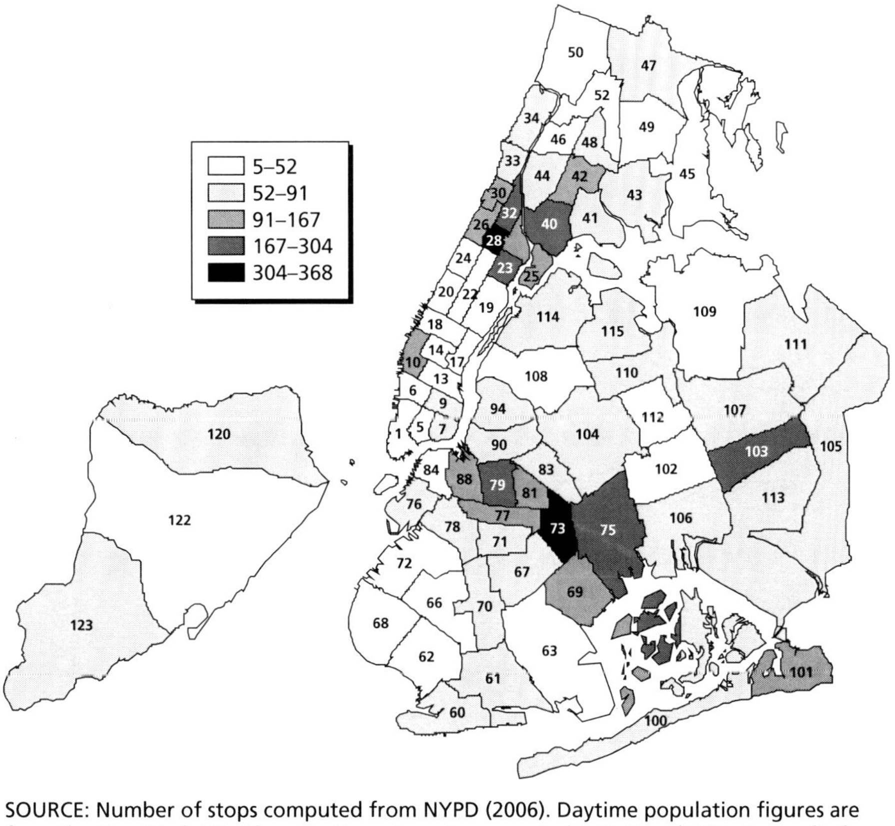

SOURCE: Number of stops computed from NYPD (2006). Daytime population figures are from the New York City Planning Department as reported in Spitzer (1999, Appendix I).
RAND *TR534-2.1*

The reasons listed for these stops are numerous. They range from suspicion of minor offenses, such as scalping tickets, riding a bicycle on the sidewalk, and sales of untaxed cigarettes,[1] to more serious suspected crimes, such as surveillance for terrorism, murder, and assault. Figure 2.2 shows the number of stops by race of the suspect for the seven most common suspected crimes. These seven reasons comprise 87 percent of all of the stops. The percentage listed under each suspected crime indicates that crime's share of the total number of stops.

Figure 2.2 raises several important issues. First, black pedestrians bore the greatest burden of stops of any group in six of the top seven stop categories (burglary being the only exception, by a small margin). This statistic raises the issue of whether black pedestrians are targeted unfairly for pedestrian stops and are therefore the victims of racial discrimination. Identifying racial discrimination is an analytic challenge—one that has received the attention of the National Academies (Blank, Dabady, and Citro, 2004). Analysis in subsequent sections will attempt to address this issue with a series of carefully constructed comparisons.

Second, judging by the height of the bars in Figure 2.2, the total number of stops appears to be quite large. The total number of stops implies roughly six stops for every 100 residents of New York City, about the same number even after accounting for the increase in New York's daytime population.[2] The Bureau of Justice Statistics (BJS) periodically conducts national surveys on contacts between the police and members of the public. The most recent report

Figure 2.2
Seven Most Common Suspected Crimes Reported as Reason for the Stop, by Race

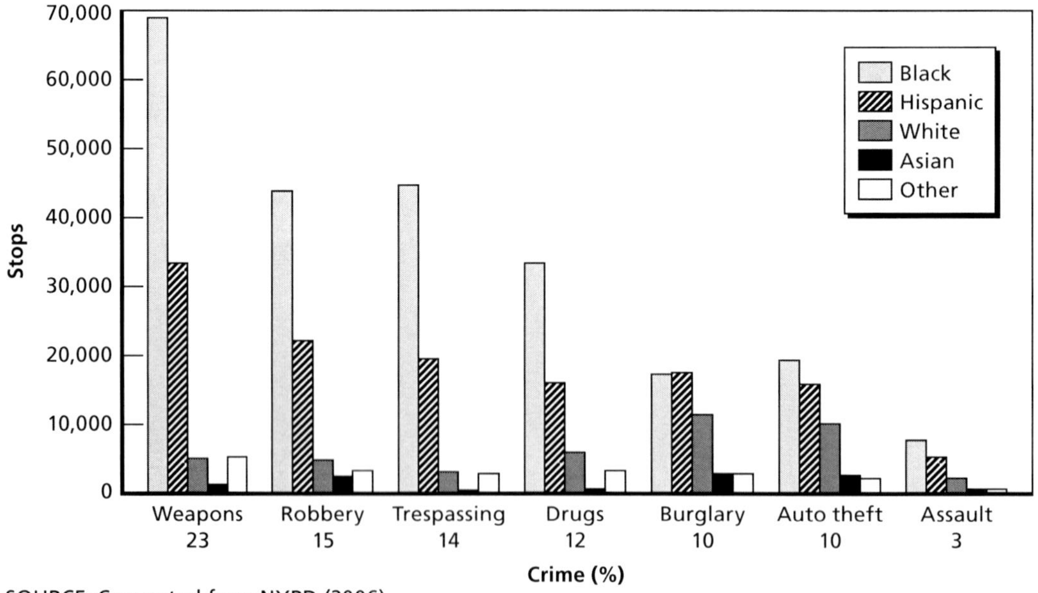

SOURCE: Computed from NYPD (2006).
RAND *TR534-2.2*

---

[1] Although officers may initiate contact with ticket scalpers, sidewalk cyclists, and untaxed cigarette vendors, such stops technically do not require an officer to complete a UF250, since they do not rise to the level of a suspected felony or penal-law misdemeanor.

[2] The U.S. Census Bureau estimates that New York City's daytime population due to regular workers commuting into New York City is about 7 percent larger than its residential population (U.S. Census Bureau, 2007).

(Durose, Smith, and Langan, 2005) indicates that 19 percent of the public had some contact with the police during a one-year period, although 41 percent of those encounters were the result of traffic stops, which UF250s do not document. The BJS data have a substantial amount of missing information, but we can use them to construct rough estimates. On average, people have 0.3 face-to-face contacts with police officers annually, about one encounter every three years. Of the respondents having had at least one face-to-face interaction with an officer, 10 to 13 percent indicated that the most recent encounter was officer initiated in a non–traffic-stop situation in which the officer was not providing the person with assistance.[3] Even with the most liberal assumptions about these rates, these statistics suggest that New York would have roughly 250,000 to 330,000 stops rather than the 500,000 stops actually recorded.[4]

There are several plausible reasons that the rate of stops with NYPD officers is so much greater than the rate suggested from our rough estimates from the BJS figures.[5] First, the estimates for daytime population used in the calculations do not account for visitors to New York City for temporary business, shopping, school, recreation, or tourism. We do not know by how much this could affect the projections. Second, New Yorkers may be more exposed to the police. New York has about 44 officers per 10,000 residents (BJS, 2007), among the largest per capita officer populations of all major cities in the United States. Nationally, the rate is 29 officers per 10,000 (Office of Justice Programs, 2006). New York also has pedestrian-traffic volume greater than that of most U.S. cities. Given the high level of exposure that New York has to police, NYPD officers are likelier to observe criminal activity when it occurs than are officers in other communities around the country. Third, while the BJS statistics are based on voluntary reports by the public, the NYPD is proactive at documenting policing activities and using that information to evaluate its policies through CompStat.[6] Officers have little disincentive to complete a UF250 even when doing so is not necessary, though some may view it as a hassle. If anything, NYPD's CompStat focus gives officers a strong incentive to generate UF250s. An officer's UF250 numbers suggest productivity. A precinct captain can use UF250 numbers to show that the precinct's officers are active in the areas that are generating complaints and where crimes occur. Officers can also use a UF250 as a record of an interaction. The last reason that the number of stops in New York is greater than the number projected from the national figures is that crime rates vary across the nation. New York, while experiencing a decrease in crime over the past several years, had a violent crime rate in 2005 of 673 per 100,000 people, compared with the national average of 469 per 100,000 (BJS, 2006). The property-crime rate (2,002 per 100,000) in New York City, however, is 42 percent below the national average of 3,430 per 100,000.

We can further consider the volume of stops by comparing it to the volume of arrests. In 2006, the NYPD received 470,000 felony and misdemeanor crime complaints, made 370,000 arrests, and issued 470,000 criminal-court summons. About 50,000 of those arrests and sum-

---

[3] The survey also asked whether the police had suspected the respondent of a crime, a more relevant question for our purposes, but only 7.5 percent of respondents with a face-to-face encounter with a police officer answered this question.

[4] The figure of 250,000 to 330,000 stops is based on a daytime population of 8.5 million × 0.3 stops per person × 10 percent or 13 percent of stops that are officer initiated and nontraffic and in which the officer was not providing a service.

[5] BJS surveyed only those older than 16 years of age, and 5 percent of NYPD's stops were under 16, so that is not likely to be a major reason.

[6] CompStat is a process that NYPD uses to regularly analyze crime issues, devise crime-reduction plans, reallocate resources, and evaluate strategies.

mons were the result of stops documented with UF250s, leaving 790,000 encounters between police and citizens in which officers observed or were responding to criminal activity that rose to the level of probable cause. While this in no way affirms that 500,000 UF250s is the right number, it is plausible that officers may have actually observed 500,000 incidents rising to the level of reasonable suspicion of a crime. Of the 506,491 stops made in 2006, 49,328 resulted in an arrest or a summons. This implies that, for every stop that resulted in an arrest or summons, there are nine stops that do not result in an arrest or summons. Given the volume of stops, this represents a large number of people who had an intrusive interaction with the police in which the police either determined that the suspect was innocent or did not have enough evidence to make an arrest. There is no objective benchmark with which to compare these numbers, as those stops not resulting in an arrest may have a valuable public-safety function, such as preventing a crime or following up on a tip. This is a matter of policing strategy that should be open to negotiation involving community representatives, elected officials, and NYPD management. It is imperative that police, in these cases in particular, communicate the reason for the stop and even proactively offer supervisor contact information to the suspect to use in the event that the suspect felt unfairly treated.

The third issue that Figure 2.2 raises is this: Weapon possession is the top reason for these encounters with police. Such stops can be evaluated to some degree based on whether a weapon was found. However, the legal grounding for frisks in *Terry v. Ohio* (88 S. Ct. 1868, 1968) gave police the right to pat down a suspect if the officer had reasonable suspicion that the individual might be armed or pose a threat to the officer's safety. In some neighborhoods, this feeling of threat to officer safety may be more pronounced than in other neighborhoods. On the other hand, the *Terry* decision does not support frisks if an officer perceives greater threats merely on the basis of a suspect's race.

For those suspects whom officers frisked (pat searches based on *Terry v. Ohio*, 88 S. Ct. 1868, 1968) or searched (based on consent or probable cause), Table 2.1 shows the frequency distribution of suspected crime and the rates of recovery of contraband (e.g., weapons, drugs, stolen property) broken down by race. Of the stops used for the analysis shown in Table 2.1, 84 percent involved frisks, 1 percent involved searches, and 15 percent involved both frisks and searches. Overall, officers are nearly twice as likely to find contraband when frisking or searching white suspects than they are when frisking or searching black suspects (6.4 percent versus 3.3 percent). However, the difference in contraband recovery rates varies by reason for the stop, with the greatest differences for stops involving suspected weapon possession and drug crimes. Since the frequency of suspected crimes for these frisks varies for black and white suspects, the overall disparity may be exaggerated by not accounting for the reason.

To account for suspected crime, we can compare the recovery rate for black suspects (3.3 percent) with what the total recovery rate for frisked white suspects would have been if their distribution of suspected crimes matched the distribution of suspected crimes of the frisked black suspects. Specifically, rather than 7 percent of frisked white suspects having the assault recovery rate of 3.4 percent, we consider what would have happened if instead 3 percent (the percentage of frisked black suspects who were suspected of assault) of the frisked white suspects had the assault recovery rate of 3.4 percent. By similarly replacing the actual frequency of each

Table 2.1
Frequency of Suspected Crimes and Recovery Rates of Contraband for Frisked or Searched Suspects, by Race

	Black		White	
Suspected Crime	**Frequency of Suspected Crime**	**Contraband Recovery Rate from Frisks and Searches**	**Frequency of Suspected Crime**	**Contraband Recovery Rate from Frisks and Searches**
Assault	3	1.9	7	3.4
Burglary	4	2.7	16	3.2
Criminal possession of a weapon (CPW)	51	2.1	28	5.0
Trespass	6	8.1	5	10.3
Drugs	10	11.1	15	16.7
Auto theft	5	3.6	15	5.9
Robbery	21	1.3	14	2.0
Total	100	3.3	100	6.4

SOURCE: Computed from NYPD (2006).

suspected crime for frisked white suspects with the frequency observed for frisked black suspects, we find the adjusted recovery rate for whites to be 5.8.[7] This implies that part of the gap between the 3.3 percent recovery rate for black suspects and the 6.4 percent recovery rate for white suspects is due not to race but rather to differences in suspected crimes.

Critical in all evaluations of the stop data is the understanding that comparisons based on raw figures ignore basic differences in the situations in which the stops occur. Within the stop-reason categories shown in Table 2.1, substantial differences persist, but other factors not included in Table 2.1, such as time, place, and age of the suspect, may further explain the gap. "Analysis of Hit Rates" in Chapter Five of this report uses statistical methods to account for several of these important factors and many more and finds a rate of contraband recovery of 3.8 percent for frisked white suspects adjusted to have stop features similar to the frisked black suspects (see Table 5.5), nearly but not completely eliminating the observed racial disparities in recovery rates.

---

[7] Computed as 0.03 × 3.4% + 0.04 × 3.2% + 0.51 × 5.0% + 0.06 × 10.3% + 0.10 × 16.7% + 0.05 × 5.9% + 0.21 × 2.0% = 5.8%.

CHAPTER THREE

External Benchmarking for the Decision to Stop

Summary

This chapter compares the racial distribution of stopped pedestrians to the racial distribution of the residential census, arrestees, and criminal suspects. External benchmarking is fraught with challenges, and the conclusions from these analyses are highly sensitive to the choice of the benchmark.

Benchmarks based on crime-suspect descriptions may provide a good measure of the rates of participation in certain types of crimes by race, but being a valid benchmark requires that suspects, regardless of race, are equally exposed to police officers.

We found that black pedestrians were stopped at a rate that is 20 to 30 percent lower than their representation in crime-suspect descriptions. Hispanic pedestrians were stopped disproportionately more, by 5 to 10 percent, than their representation among crime-suspect descriptions would predict.

We provide comparisons with several other benchmarks to demonstrate the sensitivity of external benchmarking. The arrest benchmark has been featured prominently in previous analyses of NYPD stop patterns (Spitzer, 1999; Gelman, Fagan, and Kiss, 2007). However, arrests may not accurately reflect the types of suspicious activity that officers might observe.

Black pedestrians were stopped at nearly the same rate as their representation among arrestees would suggest. Hispanic suspects appear to be stopped at a rate slightly higher (6 percent higher) than their representation among arrestees.

The most widely used, but least reliable, benchmark is the residential census. Census benchmarks do not account for differential rates of crime participation by race or for differential exposure to the police. Comparisons to the residential census are not suitable for assessing racial bias.

Black pedestrians were stopped at a rate that is 50 percent greater than their representation in the residential census. The stop rate for Hispanic pedestrians equaled their residential-census representation.

Introduction

In 2006, 53 percent of NYPD pedestrian stops involved black suspects, 29 percent Hispanic, 11 percent white, and 3 percent Asian, and race was unknown for the remaining 4 percent of the stops. A legitimate question is whether NYPD stops should have this representation of the various race groups and whether the large fraction of nonwhites among those stops suggests racial bias. *External benchmarking* describes an analysis that compares the racial distribution of the stops to the racial distribution of another source believed to represent the population at risk of being stopped by police, assuming no bias. In this chapter, we discuss issues with external benchmarking and evaluate several benchmark choices, including the residential census, arrests from 2005, and crime-suspect descriptions.

Residential Census

Historically, a common practice for judging racial fairness in police stops has been to compare the racial distribution of stops to the racial distribution of the jurisdiction's residents as reported in the decennial census. Table 3.1 indicates that blacks are overrepresented in stops by NYPD officers compared with their representation in the census. Whites and Asians are underrepresented.

The numbers in Table 3.1 show disparity and thus may cause concern. However, the census benchmarking method has been widely criticized by social scientists (see Fridell, 2004). The people who live in New York City are not at equal risk of being stopped by police even in an unbiased world. As a result, the residential population is a couple of steps removed from our ideal benchmark. Several factors could produce these disparities. The disparities could be produced by race bias—an increased tendency, whether intentional or unintentional, for officers to detain black pedestrians. Officers may view a black pedestrian with greater suspicion than they would a white pedestrian in the same situation.

Other factors are also plausible in explaining the disparities. For instance, a second factor that may account for some of the differences in Table 3.1 involves differential exposure to the police. The police have allocated their patrols to focus on areas that they view as having the greatest needs, due to the volume of crime, the number of calls for services, requests from residents and businesses, or risk assessments. The NYPD partitions the city into 76 precincts.[1] Many of the precincts with a large allocation of patrol officers also have large nonwhite populations. If an unbiased police force has 100 officers in a precinct of 1,000 residents with 90 percent nonwhite population and 20 officers in another precinct of the same number of residents

Table 3.1
Results of a Residential-Census Benchmark Analysis

Measure	Asian	Black	Hispanic	White
NYPD stops (%)	3	55	31	11
New York City census (%)	12	24	28	35
Representation in stops relative to the census	0.2	2.3	1.1	0.3
Representation in stops relative to the census (adjusting for precinct)	0.4	1.5	1.0	0.4

SOURCE: Number of stops computed from NYPD (2006), excluding those with race missing. Census data taken from U.S. Census Bureau (2007, data for 2005).

[1] Our external benchmark analyses use data at the precinct level, since arrest data and crime-suspect descriptions were readily available at the precinct level.

with 30 percent nonwhites, then collectively we would expect 80 percent of stops to involve nonwhites,[2] even though the nonwhites compose 60 percent of the community.[3] This is a well-known phenomenon in statistics called Simpson's paradox. It implies that looking at citywide aggregate comparisons can confound the comparison and that an analysis that accounts for neighborhood characteristics is essential. In addition to police allocation, there may be differences between the residential population and those on the streets exposed to the police. The racial distribution of people coming into neighborhoods for work, shopping, or entertainment can differ markedly from the racial distribution of those living in the neighborhood. Therefore, even accounting for neighborhood in an analysis cannot overcome this problem.

Table 3.1 also shows the representation of the various racial groups relative to the census of 2000. The third row of Table 3.1 shows the ratio of the stop percentage to the race percentage. The estimates in the fourth row are derived from a statistical model that compares the racial distribution of stops and the residential racial distribution within each precinct and essentially averages the ratio of the two (see Appendix A for details of the model). Accounting for precinct shows that a large part of the difference in the racial distributions of the census and stops is attributable to precinct. Blacks appear to be stopped at a rate that is 50 percent higher than the census would predict, but others factors may account for this as well.

The third factor that may account for disparities is differential rates of criminal participation. Several studies suggest that there are differences by race in the commission of crimes. In 69 percent of violent crimes reported to NYPD, the reported suspect is black. On the other hand, while drug use varies little by race, drug choice and acquisition do vary by race and can affect exposure to the police. A national survey indicates that, in large metropolitan areas, 8.6 percent of whites, 9.7 percent of blacks, and 7.2 percent of Hispanics have used an illicit substance within the last month (National Survey on Drug Use and Health and Substance Abuse and Mental Health Services Administration, 2007). However, whites are twice as likely as blacks to abuse prescription medications, and Goode (2002) noted that black drug users and sellers are likelier to be involved in frequent, public drug transactions that increase the risk of police noticing them.

Regardless of the external benchmark selected—census, arrests, suspect descriptions, or any other—the racial composition of the stops involves the interaction of the rates of criminal participation and the racial distribution of the population that the officer encounters. To put some hypothetical numbers to this, consider an unbiased officer who makes stops only when a pedestrian matches a suspect description. This officer works in a precinct with 40 blacks matching suspect descriptions and 40 whites matching suspect descriptions. If all 40 of the white suspects stay inside, travel only by car, or avoid the specific area in which the officer patrols, then this officer will stop only black pedestrians, deviating substantially from the precinct's suspect-description benchmark of 50 percent. Even the less extreme situation, in which 20 of the white suspects are exposed to the officer, results in the officer involving blacks in 67 percent of all of that officer's stops. The suspect benchmark is valid only if the suspects from the various racial groups are equally exposed to police officers.[4] Therefore, even with unbiased officers, we cannot

[2] $(0.90\times100+0.30\times20)/120$.

[3] $(0.90\times1{,}000+0.30\times1{,}000)/2{,}000$.

[4] Formally, $P(\text{race} = R|\text{stop}) = P(\text{race} = R|\text{visible},\text{suspect}) = P(\text{visible}|\text{race} = R,\text{suspect})P(\text{race} = R|\text{suspect})/P(\text{visible}|\text{suspect})$. For the stop distribution, $P(\text{race} = R|\text{stop})$, to equal the suspect benchmark, $P(\text{race} = R|\text{suspect})$, we need $P(\text{visible}|\text{race} = R,\text{suspect}) = P(\text{visible}|\text{suspect})$. This requires that *visible* be independent of race, given that an individual is a suspect.

necessarily expect seemingly sensible external benchmarks to match the racial distribution of stops. This example effectively demonstrates that any of the external benchmarks described in this section must be viewed with caution.

The primary reason for using census data is that it is inexpensive, quick, and easy. However, for the reasons previously listed, benchmarking with census data does not help us measure racial bias. Simple refinements to the residential census are possible, such as focusing on subpopulations likeliest to be involved in crime, such as men or young adults. These may explain some of the remaining differences, but other, unmeasured factors cannot be eliminated as possible explanations. Fridell (2004) summarized the problem with using the census as a benchmark by noting that "this method does not address the alternative hypothesis that *racial/ethnic groups are not equivalent in the nature and extent of their . . . law-violating behavior*" (p. 106, emphasis in original).

Dissatisfaction with the census as a benchmark has led some researchers to develop observation benchmarks, fielding teams of observers to locations to tally the racial distribution of those observed. However, even if observers could produce an accurate benchmark for those pedestrians in the area—a challenge on its own—several issues remain. There is no reason to believe that police stops should be representative of the population in the area. Officers target behaviors that they believe indicate drug transactions, stop individuals fitting a description, and respond to calls for service. Furthermore, the courts have not consistently supported the use of observational benchmarks. *United States v. Barlow* (310 F.3d 1007, 7th Cir., 2002), a case involving profiling at an Amtrak station, rejected the benchmark, since the observations were made in a different time frame from the one in which the alleged discrimination occurred. *United States v. Alcaraz-Arellano* (302 F. Supp. 2d 1217, 1229–1232, D. Kan., 2004) rejected the benchmark, since it was developed for a general population, not those violating the law.

Arrests in 2005

Gelman, Fagan, and Kiss (2007) presented an analysis of NYPD's SQF data from January 1, 1998, to March 31, 1999. This analysis also appeared in Appendix H of the New York Attorney General's report on this issue (Spitzer, 1999). Gelman, Fagan, and Kiss quoted then–Police Commissioner Howard Safir:

> The racial/ethnic distribution of the subjects of stop and frisk reports reflects the demographics of known violent crime suspects as reported by crime victims. Similarly, the demographics of arrestees in violent crimes also correspond with the demographics of known violent crime suspects. (2007, p. 4)

Gelman, Fagan, and Kiss (2007) expressed a preference for comparing the racial distribution of stops to rates of actual crime participation. They relied on data about the races of arrestees in the previous year (1997, in their analysis) as a proxy for actual crime participation and then used the arrest data as a benchmark for the racial distribution of stops. Though such data may roughly capture the racial distribution of participation in crimes for which one is likely to be caught, they may be less applicable to situations documented in UF250s. Arrests can also take place some distance away from where the crime actually occurred. More problematic is that, if officers are racially biased, in the prior year, they will have arrested a disproportionate fraction of nonwhites, and that same bias will cause them to overstop nonwhites in the current year. Such a benchmark may actually hide bias if it exists.

We replicate the most promising statistical model from Gelman, Fagan, and Kiss (2007), described in equation 4 of their article, on the 2006 SQF data, using 2005 arrest data as a benchmark. This model can be characterized in the following way: In 2005, there was a large pool of potential arrestees with a particular racial distribution, and the 2005 arrestee data represent a sample that NYPD drew from that large pool. In 2006, there was a large pool of potential suspects with a particular racial distribution whom NYPD could have stopped; the actual stops represent a sample from that large pool. If one believes that arrestees represent a suitable benchmark for assessing stops, then one must assume that the racial distribution of the large pool of potential arrestees is the same as the racial distribution of the large pool of potential stop suspects. Gelman, Fagan, and Kiss's model tests this assumption—whether the samples drawn from these two populations (arrestees and suspects) have sufficiently similar racial distributions to indicate that the arrestee and suspect populations have the same racial distribution. Appendix A describes the Gelman statistical model in more detail.

We used Gelman's model to analyze arrest data from NYPD's Online Booking System (OLBS) extract files. We tallied, by race and precinct, the number of top charge arrests, the severest charge in an arrest for violent crime (robbery, rape, murder, or assault), the number of top charge arrests for drug crimes, and the number of top charge arrests for weapons.[5] Violent crime (18 percent), drug crime (12 percent), and weapon possession (23 percent) are among the most common suspected crimes for which NYPD officers stop suspects. We compared the racial distribution of the arrestees to the racial distribution of stops in which the suspected crime was compatible with the benchmark. That is, the racial distribution of stops for suspected drug crimes was compared to the racial distribution of arrests for drug crimes.

Figure 3.1 shows the results of the analysis. Like Spitzer (1999) and Gelman, Fagan, and Kiss (2007), we used data only on black, Hispanic, and white suspects, since other racial groups had counts that were too small for statistical analysis. The top three bars indicate the rate of stops (for any reason) relative to arrests (for violent crimes, weapons, property crime, or drug crime). Black suspects were stopped at nearly the same rate (1 percent less) as their representation among arrestees would suggest. The horizontal lines through the bar represent 95 percent confidence intervals that convey the uncertainty in these estimates. For black suspects, the interval intersects with zero, indicating that there is no statistical evidence that blacks are stopped at a rate different from their arrest rate. Hispanic suspects, however, appear to be stopped at a rate slightly higher (6 percent higher) than their representation among arrestees.

The second set of bars from the top compares the racial distribution of stops for suspected violent crimes with the racial distribution of those arrested for violent crimes. All of the observed differences between the stop rates and arrest rates are less than 2 percent, and none is statistically different from zero. The same is true for the third set of bars, which compares stops for suspected drug crimes with drug arrests. There appears to be no statistical evidence for a race effect, as all of the intervals intersect with zero.

The fourth set of bars from the top of Figure 3.1 compares stops for suspected criminal possession of a weapon (the most common reason for UF250s) to arrests in which the top charge was weapon possession. Officers stop black suspects for suspected weapon possession

---

[5] Those arrested for serious crimes, such as robbery, who also had a gun will have that serious crime, not a weapon offense, as the top charge.

Figure 3.1
Comparison of Stop Rates to Seven External Benchmarks

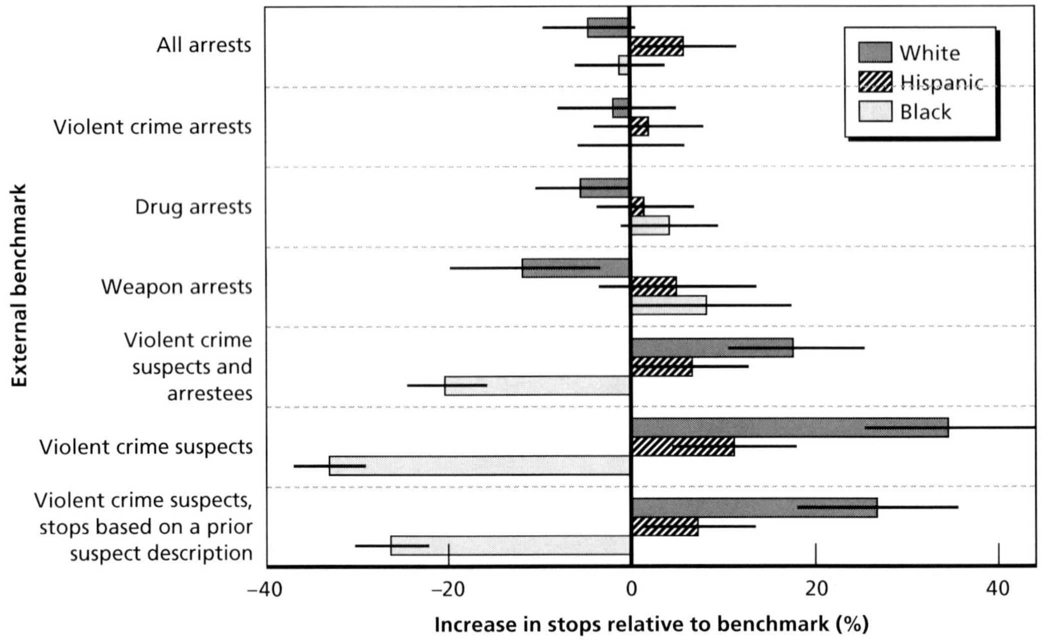

SOURCE: Computed from NYPD (2006).
NOTE: Each bar compares a race's percentage share of the pedestrian stops to its percentage share of the specified benchmark. Bars to the right of 0 indicate more stops than the benchmark would suggest, and bars to the left of 0 indicate fewer stops than the benchmark would suggest. The horizontal line through each bar represents the 95 percent confidence interval that conveys the uncertainty in these estimates.
RAND *TR534-3.1*

at a rate greater (8 percent greater) than their weapon arrest rate. White suspects, on the other hand, have a stop rate that is 11 percent lower than their weapon arrest rate. The weapon arrest benchmark is constructed from cases in which the top charge is illegal weapon possession. Robbery arrests in which the suspect has a weapon are not counted as a weapon arrest because the top charge is robbery. If white arrestees are likelier to have no other criminal involvement beyond illegal firearm possession, then their representation in the weapon arrestees might be a reasonable benchmark for stops of white pedestrians for suspected weapon possession. If black suspects are likelier to have an illegal firearm and have additional criminal involvement, then they will be underrepresented in the weapon-arrestee population, which could be one explanation for the disparity observed in Figure 3.1.

Crime-Suspect Descriptions

As the quotation from then-Commissioner Safir indicated, violent-crime suspect descriptions as reported by crime victims might be a better benchmark. This category represents the public's requests to the NYPD to look for individuals matching a certain description. In 30 percent of the stops, a call for service or a suspect description initiated the stop. During the one shift observed by a RAND researcher, all of the UF250s observed were generated as a result of calls for service or suspect descriptions.

We supplemented the arrestee data with data on suspect descriptions for violent crime in 2006 from the NYPD's complaint-report data file and compared them with stops for violent crimes. To compare the racial distribution of stops for violent crimes with the racial distribution of violent-crime suspects and arrestees, we used the same model used for the arrest benchmark described previously. We also constructed a benchmark from crime-suspect descriptions alone without arrestees. Figure 3.1 also shows the results from external benchmarks using violent-crime suspects with and without arrestees.

The bottom three sets of bars in Figure 3.1 indicate that black suspects are substantially understopped relative to their representation in crime-suspect descriptions. The inclusion or exclusion of violent-crime arrestees along with violent-crime suspects does not change this result. Overall, black suspects were described in 69 percent of all violent-crime suspect descriptions even though black pedestrians comprise 53 percent of all stops and 24 percent of the city's population. The last set of bars restricts the set of stops to only those in which the officer indicated that the suspect fit a crime-suspect description. This restriction does not change the conclusions.

Conclusions

External benchmarking is fraught with challenges. Every analysis based on external benchmarking requires careful interpretation. Most important, the method can either detect or hide racial bias due to unobserved or unmeasured factors that affect both the racial distribution that the benchmark establishes and the racial distribution of the stops. For example, drug arrests take many forms, including complex buy-bust operations, complaints from residents, and direct observation by officers. Stops documented in UF250s are generated only from the latter two situations, while the drug-arrest benchmark includes all of these arrests. Goode (2002) noted that black drug sellers and buyers are likelier to be involved in street-level sales and, therefore, have greater exposure to the police and are likelier to appear in UF250s than the arrestee benchmark might suggest.

Our analysis in this section has examined several external benchmark choices. Importantly, this chapter has shown that the conclusions from external benchmarking are highly sensitive to the choice of benchmark. In other words, the results of any analysis using external benchmarks may vary drastically depending on which benchmark is used. The residential census is a commonly attempted first-look analysis, but researchers who study racial profiling discourage its use, arguing that the people exposed to the police could be different from those who live in the neighborhood (e.g., people from outside the precinct) and noting the belief that the census tends to undercount nonwhites. The 1999 report from the New York Attorney General's office used the previous year's arrests to establish a benchmark (Spitzer, 1999). We replicated this analysis for the 2006 data with separate analyses for drug and weapon arrests. Last, we utilized data on crime-suspect descriptions, a benchmark suggested in Gelman, Fagan, and Kiss (2007).

With the exception of the residential census benchmark, the external-benchmark analysis does not indicate that black pedestrians were overstopped. Hispanic pedestrians appear to have been stopped more frequently than their representation among arrestees and crime-suspect descriptions would predict.

CHAPTER FOUR

Internal Benchmarking for the Decision to Stop

Summary

This chapter describes an analysis that compares the racial distribution of each officer's stops to a benchmark racial distribution constructed using similarly situated stops made by other officers.

Our analysis found the following:

- Five officers appear to have stopped substantially more black suspects than other officers made when patrolling the same areas, at the same times, and with the same assignment. Nine officers stopped substantially fewer black suspects than expected.
- Ten officers appear to have stopped substantially more Hispanic suspects than other officers made when patrolling the same areas, at the same times, and with the same assignment. Four officers stopped substantially fewer Hispanic suspects than expected.
- Six of the 15 flagged officers are from the Queens South borough.

Introduction

If racial bias is a result of a few problem officers, then the methods described in the previous chapter, which examine bias at the departmental level, are unlikely to detect the problem, and, even if somehow they have the statistical power to detect the problem, they cannot help to identify potential problem officers. Walker (2001, 2002, 2003) conceptualized the internal benchmark, a framework that compares officers' stop decisions with decisions made by other officers working in similar situations. We developed an internal benchmark methodology to compare the racial distribution of pedestrians whom individual police officers have stopped with that of pedestrians whom other officers in the same role have stopped at the same times and places.

While this process is useful for flagging potential problem officers, it has some drawbacks. First, if officers in the entire precinct are equally biased, the method will not flag any officers as being problematic. We must rely on other analyses to assess that issue. Second, officers whom the method flags as outliers may have legitimate explanations for the observed differences. For example, a Spanish-speaking officer may appear to make an excessive number of stops of Hispanic suspects, when, in fact, whenever the officer or the officer's partner detains a Hispanic suspect, the Spanish-speaking officer takes the lead because of language specialty and completes the UF250. Such situations should be detectable when supervisors review cases.

Otherwise, the method eliminates possible explanations based on time or place, so the range of explanations is limited.

Methods

The fundamental goal of internal benchmarking is to compare the rate of nonwhite-pedestrian stops for a particular officer with the rate of nonwhite-pedestrian stops for other officers patrolling the same area at the same time. Matching in this way assures us that the target officer and the comparison officers are exposed to the same set of offenses and offenders.

Several matching procedures have been proposed. Direct matching to construct internal benchmarks may provide an insufficient quantity of matches for some officers. To increase the set of matched officers, matching criteria might be broadened to the point at which officers are matched with officers making stops at substantially different times and places. For example, Decker and Rojek (2002) matched each St. Louis police officer to all other officers working in the same police districts. It is unclear whether matching by district alone was sufficient to ensure validity. They did not match by time of day or day of week, although they argued that officers rotated shifts sufficiently so as not to warrant concern.

But in many NYPD jurisdictions, matching by precinct alone is insufficient because the racial mix of the population and law-enforcement practices can vary substantially within a precinct. More precise measures of the location of the stop are, therefore, necessary if such propositions are true. Additionally, matching at the officer level is inappropriate because officers' assignments can vary in several ways, such as geography and time of the year. Therefore, we use a method that matches each officer's collection of stops to a collection of stops made by other officers at the same times and places. Stops were matched on month, day of week, time of day, precinct, x-y coordinates of the stop location, whether it was a transit or public-housing location, the officer's assigned command, whether the officer was in uniform, and whether the stop was a result of a radio run.

Consider Officer A, who patrols in Brooklyn North. In 2006, Officer A made 392 stops. Of those stops, 83 percent involved black suspects, and another 10 percent involved Hispanic suspects. Our internal-benchmark analysis involves comparing these numbers to the racial distribution of other officers' stops that are similar with regard to time, place, and other factors. We selected those similarly situated stops by using a method called *propensity-score weighting*. Propensity-score weighting allows us to characterize the stops made by other officers in a way that provides a useful comparison to the distribution of the stop features for an individual officer (see Appendix B for details). For Officer A, the method effectively identified 3,676 similarly situated stops made by other officers. These stops were selected as the benchmark group for Officer A because they were similar to Officer A's stops in terms of when they occurred (e.g., date, time of day), where they occurred (e.g., precinct, x-y coordinates), the assigned command of the officer making the stop, whether the officer making the stop was in uniform, and whether the stop was a result of a radio call. Figure 4.1 and Table 4.1 demonstrate that this collection of 3,676 is nearly identical to the officer's stops in several respects.

The map shown in the left panel of Figure 4.1 indicates the locations of this officer's stops in 2006. The contour lines mark a region in the southern end of the 79th precinct, where the majority of the stops occurred. The map shown in the right panel indicates the locations of the 3,676 similarly situated stops selected to match the officer's stops. In addition to matching

Figure 4.1
Maps of the Sample Officer's Stops and of Similarly Situated Stops Made by Other Officers

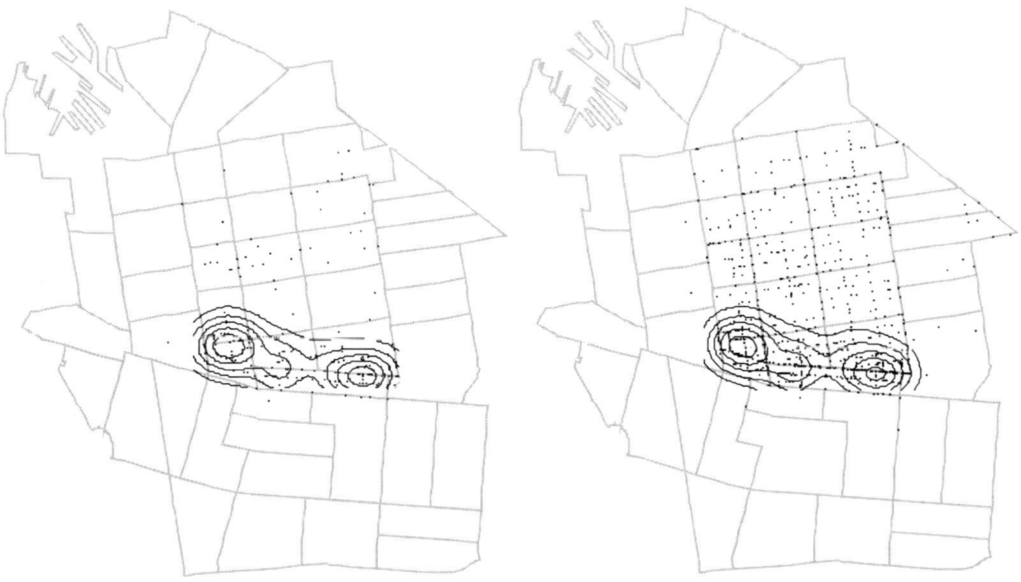

SOURCE: Computed from NYPD (2006).
NOTE: The left map shows the sample officer's stops; the right map shows similarly situated stops made by other officers. The contours indicate the regions of the maps with the highest concentrations of stops.
RAND *TR534-4.1*

the precinct in which the officer works, the contours in the right panel show that the matched stops used for constructing the internal benchmark also occurred in the southern end of the precinct. Any differences between the racial distribution of suspects involved in the officer's stops and the racial distribution of the matched stops cannot be due to location.

While Figure 4.1 demonstrates that effective matching by location is possible, the method simultaneously matches on numerous other attributes. All of these other attributes, such as time of the stop, can also be incorporated in the propensity-score weighting. Table 4.1 demonstrates that we can also select stops that match Officer A's stops by month, day of the week, time of day, additional location details, the officer's assignment (NYPD command), the frequency with which the officer is in uniform, and the frequency with which the officer's stops are a result of radio runs (calls for service). These matches are simultaneous. That is, the same collection of 3,676 stops made by the other officers matches the distribution of features of the officer in question.

Some features are not perfectly balanced in Table 4.1, such as the frequency of being in uniform and being on a radio run. We accounted for these slight differences using regression adjustment, a standard statistical practice for further removing chance differences among groups (Kang and Schafer, 2007).

For several reasons, the internal benchmark does not match officers on the reason for the stop. First, officers patrolling the same areas at the same times should be exposed to similar suspicious activity. However, for the sample officer in Table 4.1, the crimes suspected in the officer's stops are quite different from those in the benchmark, as shown in Table 4.2. Most noticeably, the sample officer frequently recorded suspected drug sales as the suspected crime, while similarly situated officers more evenly split suspected drug crimes between possession

Table 4.1
Construction of an Internal Benchmark for a Sample Officer

Stop Characteristic		Officer A (%) (N = 392)	Internal Benchmark (%) (N = 3,676)
Month	January	3	3
	February	4	4
	March	8	9
	April	7	5
	May	12	12
	June	9	9
	July	7	7
	August	8	9
	September	10	10
	October	11	10
	November	11	11
	December	9	10
Day of the week	Monday	13	13
	Tuesday	11	10
	Wednesday	14	15
	Thursday	22	21
	Friday	15	16
	Saturday	10	11
	Sunday	15	14
Time of day	[12–2 a.m.]	11	11
	(2–4 a.m.]	5	5
	(10 a.m. –12 p.m.]	0	1
	(12–2 p.m.]	12	13
	(2–4 p.m.]	13	12
	(4–6 p.m.]	9	10
	(6–8 p.m.]	8	8
	(8–10 p.m.]	23	23
	(10 p.m. –12 a.m.]	17	17
Patrol borough	Brooklyn North	100	100
Precinct	77	0	0
	79	98	98
	81	1	1
	88	1	0

Table 4.1—Continued

Stop Characteristic		Officer A (%) (N = 392)	Internal Benchmark (%) (N = 3,676)
Inside or outside	Inside	4	6
	Outside	96	94
Housing or transit	Transit	0	0
	Housing	0	0
	Other	100	100
Command	79th precinct	100	100
In uniform	Yes	99	97
	No	1	3
Radio run	Yes	1	3
	No	99	97

SOURCE: Computed from NYPD (2006).

NOTE: The numbers in the table indicate the percentage of stops having that feature.

and sale. They may have been observing the same kinds of suspicious activity but simply categorizing differently. Second, while officers have some discretion as to what suspicious activity to investigate, the selectively targeting or avoiding of certain types of suspect crimes can have disparate impact on the racial makeup of stopped suspects. Rather than having the internal benchmark match on the stop reasons, NYPD can evaluate the stop reasons for those officers who are flagged as stopping a disproportionate fraction of nonwhites. In addition to assessing issues of racial profiling, supervisors can evaluate whether the officer's stop patterns are consistent with precinct priorities.

In 2006, 3,034 officers completed more than 50 UF250s, the minimum number of stops for which we could accurately establish an internal benchmark. For each officer, in turn, we constructed a separate internal benchmark like the one shown in Table 4.1, one specifically tailored for each officer's patterns of stops. For 278 of those officers, a suitable set of comparison-group stops could not be constructed. The best set of comparison-group stops differed from

Table 4.2
Comparison of the Percentage of Stops for a Particular Suspected Crime for the Sample Officer and the Officer's Internal Benchmark

Crime Suspected	Sample Officer's Stops (%)	Benchmark Stops (%)
Criminal trespass	4	2
Burglary	13	13
Weapon possession	3	13
Robbery	15	14
Drug possession	6	27
Drug sale	47	20

SOURCE: Computed from NYPD (2006).

the officer's stops by more than 10 percent on some factors. These officers generally made few stops, scattered across numerous precincts and even multiple boroughs, in a variety of roles (e.g., transit police, sometimes in uniform). Our final set for analysis includes 2,756 officers.[1] These officers collectively made 54 percent of the stops.

For the sample officer's benchmark, 78 percent of the 3,676 benchmark stops involved black suspects, and 9 percent involved Hispanic suspects, a lower rate of nonwhite-pedestrian stops than the officer's stop pattern of 83 percent black and 10 percent Hispanic. Our analysis focuses on comparisons of the rate of black and Hispanic suspects, since the rates of other nonwhite groups were generally too small. The remaining question is whether this difference presents a large disparity. Chance differences are likely, especially when the stops are few. Statistical measures that account for the number of stops are useful for setting appropriate cutoffs.

The z-statistic is the commonly used statistical measure for assessing the magnitude of the difference between an officer's nonwhite-pedestrian–stop fraction and the officer's internal benchmark (Fridell, 2004). The z-statistic scales the difference to account for the number of stops that the officer made and the number of stops used to construct the internal benchmark, so that large differences based on a small number of stops are treated with greater uncertainty than large differences based on a large number of stops. Given the value of an officer's z-statistic, we can estimate the probability that a flagged officer is, in fact, an outlier. We flagged all officers with an outlier probability exceeding 50 percent. The choice of 50 percent leads to a z-statistic cutoff of about 5.0 for the black-suspect internal benchmark and a cutoff of 4.0 for the Hispanic-suspect internal benchmark. That cutoff is subjective and depends on the costs associated with failing to flag a problem officer and the costs associated with investigating each flagged officer. The commonly selected cutoff is 80 percent (Efron, 2004), but we believed that such a choice would undervalue the cost of failing to identify a problem officer. In addition, the 50 percent probability cutoff produces a short list of officers for closer evaluation. Appendix C contains technical details about the methodology.

Results

Figure 4.2 shows a histogram of the 2,756 results from an internal-benchmark analysis for the rate of black-suspect stops. The arrows mark the cutoff at which the probability of being an outlier exceeds 50 percent. The five blocks at the extreme right of the histogram represent five officers who overstopped black suspects relative to similarly situated stops made by other officers. The analysis flags a total of nine officers in the extreme left tail of the histogram for greatly understopping black suspects relative to their internal benchmark.

---

[1] All RAND studies go before an institutional review board that reviews research involving human subjects, as required by federal regulations. RAND's Federalwide Assurance for the Protection of Human Subjects (NIH, through 2010) serves as its assurance of compliance with the regulations of 16 federal departments and agencies. According to this assurance, the committee is responsible for review regardless of source of funding. These federal regulations prevent RAND research from singling out specific individuals whom its research could adversely affect. The analysis in this section offers an estimate of the number of the NYPD's patrol officers of concern, but RAND cannot identify individual officers. For the Cincinnati Police Department, RAND has transferred the analytical capabilities to the department's analysts so that they can properly review their officers. A similar arrangement may be possible with NYPD.

Figure 4.2
Distribution of 2,756 Officer-Level Analyses

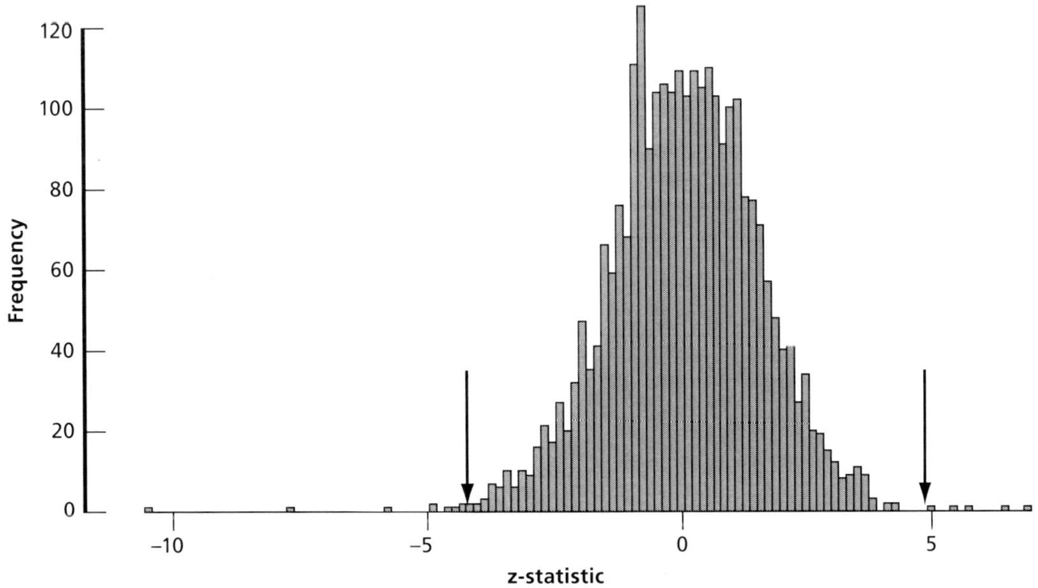

SOURCE: Computed from NYPD (2006).
NOTE: Each bar represents the number of officers having the z-statistic specified on the horizontal axis. The arrows mark the cutoff at which the probability of being an outlier exceeds 50 percent.
RAND *TR534-4.2*

Table 4.3 describes the features of the flagged officers' stops in greater detail. The first five rows correspond to those officers with a percentage of stops involving black suspects (shown in the second column) that greatly exceeds the calculated benchmark (column three). Column four and five, respectively, indicate the number of stops the officer made and the number of stops composing the benchmark. Since the comparison-group stops are weighted to make their features align with the officer's stop features, we used the effective sample size[2] to measure the number of comparison-group stops.

The last column of Table 4.3 shows the estimated probability that the officer's stop pattern is an outlier and that the observed differences are not simply due to chance. All of the probabilities for the officers that appear to have overstopped black suspects are well in excess of 50 percent. While there may be a reason aside from racial bias that could explain these differences, the analysis has eliminated all of the reasons listed in Table 4.1, such as time and place, and the calculated probabilities indicate that it is unlikely that the differences are due to chance.

The bottom nine rows of Table 4.3 show stop information for the nine officers who are substantially understopping black suspects relative to similarly situated stops.

The stops that these officers make consist of a mixture of low- and high-discretion stops. We reran the internal benchmark excluding stops resulting from calls for service and those based on suspect descriptions, those that offer the least opportunity for officers to express any racial biases. This focused the analysis on those stops for which racial bias is likelier to have

---

[2] The effective sample size is the number of observations from a simple random sample needed to obtain an estimate of the race effect with precision equal to the precision obtained with the weighted comparison observations.

Table 4.3
Internal-Benchmark Analysis for Stop Rates of Black Suspects

Measure	Black (%)		Stops		Outlier probability
	Officer	Benchmark	Officer	Benchmark	
Stop rate of black suspects in excess of the benchmark	86	55	151	773	97[a]
	85	67	218	473	62[a]
	77	56	237	1,081	86
	75	51	178	483	78
	64	20	59	695	98
Stop rate of black suspects less than the benchmark	57	79	152	1,593	89
	56	80	63	304	51
	49	74	94	621	70
	46	77	61	633	70
	42	80	99	872	>99
	36	87	92	1,696	>99
	19	56	53	679	62
	17	49	65	355	55[a]
	8	39	71	291	52[a]

SOURCE: Computed from NYPD (2006).

NOTE: Each row represents one officer and reports the statistics pertaining to that officer.

[a] These officers also appear in Table 4.4.

an impact. Out of 1,910 officers for whom we could construct good internal benchmarks, the reanalysis flagged two officers, both of whom already appear in Table 4.3.

Table 4.4 shows the analysis that identified officers who appear to have overstopped Hispanic suspects and flagged nine officers for overstopping Hispanics. Three officers appear to have been substantially understopping Hispanics. Four of the officers listed in Table 4.4 also appear in Table 4.3; they are marked in both tables. One officer's pattern of overstopping black suspects (86 percent black, shown in Table 4.3) has the effect of reducing the officer's rate of stopping Hispanics (11 percent Hispanic, shown in Table 4.4). A similar effect occurs for two of the officers who appear to have been overstopping Hispanics.

Table 4.5 shows the results from rerunning the internal benchmark excluding stops based on suspect descriptions and stops resulting from calls for service. Most of the officers flagged from this analysis also appear in Table 4.4. However, the analysis also flagged two additional officers, one for overstopping Hispanics and another for substantially understopping Hispanics relative to their internal benchmark.

We also attempted an analysis to determine whether officers targeted nonwhite pedestrians generally. This analysis was problematic, since there are few white suspects in the data. Fifteen percent of the officers stopped no white suspects, but all of the benchmarks for these officers had the expected fraction of nonwhites stopped greater than 90 percent, most of them exceeding 97 percent. For those officers who did not stop only nonwhites, 121 of them

Table 4.4
Internal-Benchmark Analysis for Stop Rates of Hispanic Suspects

	Hispanic (%)		Stops		
Measure	**Officer**	**Benchmark**	**Officer**	**Benchmark**	**Outlier Probability**
Stop rate of Hispanic suspects in excess of the benchmark	86	52	71	291	72[a]
	80	43	65	355	83[a]
	48	24	122	194	65
	44	21	97	396	65
	43	20	84	1,294	65
	42	23	113	1,493	59
	29	10	77	1,100	77
	22	3	82	139	>99
	14	2	200	510	>99
Stop rate of Hispanic suspects less than the benchmark	14	43	84	431	52
	11	38	151	773	98[a]
	7	26	218	473	92[a]

SOURCE: Computed from NYPD (2006).

NOTE: Each row represents one officer and reports the statistics pertaining to that officer.

[a] These officers also appear in Table 4.3.

Table 4.5
Internal-Benchmark Analysis for Stop Rates of Hispanic Suspects, Excluding Stops Based on Suspect Descriptions or Calls for Service

	Hispanic (%)		Stops		
Measure	**Officer**	**Benchmark**	**Officer**	**Benchmark**	**Outlier probability**
Stop rate of Hispanic suspects in excess of the benchmark	86	51	70	266	91[a]
	80	44	65	336	92[a]
	46	22	91	635	88[a]
	45	20	78	1,310	92[a]
	38	16	72	488	71
Stop rate of Hispanic suspects less than the benchmark	24	54	90	171	65
	7	26	203	652	94[a]

SOURCE: Computed from NYPD (2006).

NOTE: Each row represents one officer and reports the statistics pertaining to that officer.

[a] These officers also appear in Table 4.4.

understopped nonwhites relative to their benchmark, and only one appeared to overstop nonwhites, with a nonwhite-pedestrian stop rate of 50 percent relative to a benchmark of 32 percent.

No obvious patterns emerged from the features of the 15 officers who overstopped either black or Hispanic suspects relative to their benchmark. Six of the officers were from the Queens South borough, a statistically disproportionate number, given that 12 percent of the stop activity occurred in Queens South. The remaining nine officers were distributed fairly uniformly across the boroughs. Twelve of the officers were precinct patrol officers, two were public-housing officers, and one was assigned to an anticrime unit.

Conclusions

The internal-benchmark analysis flagged five officers among those making at least 50 pedestrian stops who were substantially overstopping black suspects and 10 officers who were substantially overstopping Hispanic suspects. In addition, nine other officers were substantially understopping nonwhites. At this stage, we do not know whether there is a problem with these officers, but we have removed numerous plausible explanations for the difference, including chance differences and differences in time and place. We encourage NYPD supervisors to identify and follow up on flagged officers to evaluate other plausible reasons for the disparity. The method implemented for the analysis in this chapter eliminates the obvious explanations that are based on time, place, or assignment, so discussions between supervisors and the flagged officers must delve more deeply than these reasons.

As for the public's concern about problem officers, the internal-benchmark analysis has flagged 0.5 percent of the 2,756 NYPD officers most active in pedestrian-stop activity. Those 2,756 most active officers, about 7 percent of the total number of officers, account for 54 percent of the total number of 2006 stops. The remaining stops were made by another 15,855 officers, for whom an accurate internal benchmark could not be constructed, mostly because they conducted too few stops. While the data suggest that only a small fraction of the officers most active in pedestrian stops may be outliers, the stops made by the 15,855 stops that we could not analyze may still be of concern. Racial bias in their SQF behavior may collectively reveal itself in post-stop analyses of frisks, searches, uses of force, and arrests.

CHAPTER FIVE

Analysis of Post-Stop Outcomes

Summary

This chapter assesses racial disparities with regard to activities that occur after a stop is made, including frisks, searches, uses of force, and arrests.

Our analysis found the following:

- Officers frisked white suspects slightly less frequently than they did *similarly situated* nonwhites (29 percent of stops versus 33 percent of stops). Black suspects were slightly likelier to have been frisked than white suspects stopped in circumstances similar to the black suspects (46 percent versus 42 percent). While there is a gap, this difference is much smaller than what the aggregate statistics indicated.
- The rates of searches were nearly equal across racial groups, between 6 and 7 percent. However, in Staten Island, the rate of searching nonwhite suspects was significantly greater than that of searching white suspects.
- White suspects were slightly likelier to be issued a summons than were similarly situated nonwhite suspects (5.7 percent versus 5.2 percent). On the other hand, arrest rates for white suspects were slightly lower than those for similarly situated nonwhites (4.8 percent versus 5.1 percent).
- Officers were slightly less likely to use force against white suspects than they were to use it against similarly situated nonwhites (15 percent versus 16 percent); however, in Queens, Brooklyn North, and the Bronx, there was no evidence that use-of-force rates varied across races.
- Officers recovered contraband (such as weapons, illegal drugs, or stolen property) in 6.4 percent of the stops of white suspects. The contraband recovery rate was 5.7 percent for similarly situated black suspects and 5.4 percent for similarly situated Hispanic suspects.

Introduction

At first glance, the raw statistics indicate large racial disparities in the outcomes of stops. For example, in Manhattan South, 29 percent of stopped white pedestrians were frisked, compared with 38 percent of nonwhites whom officers stopped. Differences of similar magnitude occurred in other boroughs as well on other stop outcomes, such as use of force. These stark differences are cause for concern but require closer inspection.

Our first finding is that pedestrians of various racial groups were stopped at different times and places and for different reasons. This is not surprising—census data indicate, and

New York residents know, that certain neighborhoods have concentrations of different races. Even within an NYPD precinct, the residential racial distributions vary greatly. Furthermore, economists have documented that work hours can vary greatly by race (Hamermesh, 1996), which affects the racial distribution of pedestrians exposed to the police at various times of the day. Figure 2.2 in Chapter Two also showed that the reasons for the stops vary substantially by race. As a result, some of the observed differences in stop outcomes could be attributable to time, place, and reason for which the stop occurred.

The analysis described in this chapter made comparisons between white and nonwhite pedestrians who were stopped in similar situations, in the same places, at the same times, and for the same reasons. By comparing similarly situated pedestrians, the analysis removed many alternative explanations for any observed differences. We also compared stops of black pedestrians to similarly situated white, Hispanic, and all nonblack pedestrians.

Methods

Table 5.1 uses Manhattan South as an example and shows that white and nonwhite pedestrians were stopped under different circumstances. The first two columns list a variety of stop features. The third column of the table shows the percentage of the stopped white pedestrians whose stops had a particular feature. For example, 20 percent of the stopped white pedestrians were stopped in the 14th precinct, which includes Penn Station, Times Square, Madison Square Garden, and the New York Public Library. Of the nonwhites stopped in Manhattan South, 28 percent were stopped in the 14th, as shown in the last column, "Nonwhite (unadjusted)." When compared with nonwhite pedestrians, white pedestrians were also likelier to be stopped for burglary and drug possession, to have a physical form of identification, or to be stopped as a result of a radio run, but they were less likely to be stopped by housing and transit police and slightly less likely to be stopped in the early afternoon. It is possible that bias causes some of the differences in when, where, and why these stops occurred. However, this chapter focuses on detecting biases after these stop decisions have already been made.

To isolate the effect of racial bias, we must adjust for all factors associated with both race and post-stop outcomes, and we have made a concerted effort to include all such observable features in this analysis. The main issue identified in Table 5.1 is that differences by race in the rates of frisks and searches may be due to differences in when, where, and why the stops occurred. These factors may, independently of race, influence an officer's post-stop decision-making process. Suspicion of weapon possession, for example, should almost always result in a frisk.

To ensure a fair comparison, we matched similarly situated white and nonwhite pedestrians and compared their stop outcomes. The column labeled "Nonwhite (adjusted)" in Table 5.1 shows the results of a propensity-score weighting technique (Ridgeway, 2006) that reweights the stops involving nonwhite pedestrians so that they have the same distribution of features as those involving white pedestrians. The technique adjusts for the stopping of nonwhite pedestrians at times, in places, and for reasons that are atypical of stopped white pedestrians. Simultaneously, stops of nonwhite pedestrians that have features similar to stops of white pedestrians are given more weight. As a result, the percentages shown in the "White" and the "Nonwhite (adjusted)" columns are nearly identical. Any differences in search rates, for example, cannot be due to differences in any of the features listed in Table 5.1. Arriving at this near match

Table 5.1
Distribution of Stop Features, by Race, for Manhattan South

		Stopped Pedestrians		
Stop Feature		**White (N = 5,547)**	**Nonwhite (adjusted) (N = 9,781)**	**Nonwhite (unadjusted) (N = 31,716)**
Crime suspected (%)	Assault	7	7	6
	Burglary	15	15	7
	CPW	9	10	11
	Drugs	5	5	3
	Trespass	6	7	9
	Grand larceny	9	10	14
	Grand larceny, auto (GLA)	5	5	4
	Petit larceny	6	6	9
	Robbery	5	5	11
Precinct (%)	1	6	6	5
	5	7	8	9
	6	9	9	7
	7	8	8	12
	9	14	14	12
	10	9	9	8
	13	9	9	9
	14	20	20	28
	17	8	8	3
	18	9	9	8
Average age (years)		33	33	32
Time of day (%)	[12–4 a.m.]	24	23	18
	(4–8 a.m.]	8	8	6
	(8 a.m.–12 p.m.]	11	11	10
	(12–4 p.m.]	16	16	21
	(4–8 p.m.]	20	20	23
	(8 p.m.–12 a.m.]	21	21	21
Location (%)	Housing	4	5	14
	Transit	22	22	36
	Other	74	73	50

Table 5.1—Continued

Stop Feature		Stopped Pedestrians: White (N = 5,547)	Nonwhite (adjusted) (N = 9,781)	Nonwhite (unadjusted) (N = 31,716)
Month (%)	January	10	9	9
	February	8	8	8
	March	9	9	9
	April	8	9	8
	May	9	8	8
	June	7	7	7
	July	8	8	8
	August	9	9	10
	September	8	8	9
	October	9	9	9
	November	8	8	8
	December	7	7	7
Male (%)		88	88	91
Day of the week (%)	Sunday	13	13	11
	Monday	10	11	11
	Tuesday	16	17	17
	Wednesday	16	17	18
	Thursday	16	16	17
	Friday	15	14	15
	Saturday	14	13	12
Type of ID (%)	Physical	64	63	56
	Verbal	30	31	37
Radio run (%)	Yes	21	21	13

SOURCE: Computed from NYPD (2006).

NOTE: The stop features are sorted by how much the stopped white and nonwhite pedestrians differed with regard to that feature. The levels of crime suspected shown are limited to those representing at least 5 percent of the stops.

on the distribution of stop features required effectively paring the set of 31,716 stops of nonwhite pedestrians in Manhattan South down to 9,781 comparable stops. We repeated this process, separately matching black and Hispanic pedestrians to have the same distribution of stop features as the white pedestrians had. Appendix B provides technical details on this methodology.

In addition to the stop features listed in Table 5.1, we matched white and nonwhite pedestrians on 20 other features: the x-y coordinates of the stop location, being reported by witness, being part of an ongoing investigation, being in a high-crime area, being at a high-crime time of day, being close to the scene of an incident, detecting sights and sounds of criminal activity, evasiveness, association with known criminals, changing direction at the sight of an officer, carrying a suspicious object, fitting a suspect description, appearing to be casing, acting as a lookout, wearing clothes consistent with those commonly used in crime, making furtive movements, acting in a manner consistent with a drug transaction or a violent crime, or having a suspicious bulge.

For each of the eight patrol boroughs, we selected a matched set of black, Hispanic, and all nonwhite (composed of black, Hispanic, Asian, and other nonwhite races) pedestrians with the same distribution of features as the stopped white pedestrians had in that borough. We then compared the two groups in terms of the rates of frisk, search, summon, arrest, and use of force.

Since the analysis reweights the black-, Hispanic-, and all-nonwhite-pedestrian stops to have the same stop features as those of white pedestrians, this analysis addresses only whether there is racial bias in the contexts (times, places, and reasons) in which white pedestrians are stopped. If bias occurs largely in the contexts in which black pedestrians are stopped, then even the white-black comparison will misrepresent the problem. In response to this issue, we repeated the analysis by comparing the outcomes of stops of black pedestrians with similarly situated stops of Hispanic, white, and nonblack (Asian, Hispanic, white, and all other nonblack races) pedestrians. This latter analysis addresses whether there is differential treatment at the times and places at which stops of black pedestrians generally occur.

Results

Table 5.2 shows the results of the analysis comparing stops of white pedestrians with similarly situated stops of nonwhites. The stops of nonwhites tend to be slightly more intrusive than those of similarly situated white suspects. For example, stopped nonwhites have a frisk rate that is about 3 to 4 percent higher than that for white pedestrians. These estimates have sufficient precision to conclude that the differences are not chance differences. Search rates appear to be similar between white- and nonwhite-pedestrian stops, though search rates in Staten Island were slightly elevated for nonwhites, particularly for black pedestrians.

In three of the patrol boroughs, white suspects were slightly likelier to be issued a summons than were similarly situated nonwhites (5.7 percent versus 5.2 percent). One possible reason for this is that the stopped white suspects might be likelier to be involved in criminal activity, but other explanations are possible. Officers might have made some stops of nonwhites based on weaker evidence and, therefore, believed that prosecution for those suspected crimes is less likely to succeed. However, the absolute difference in rates is small enough to suggest that such a biased practice could not have been frequently applied, if at all. A third possible explanation based on previous analysis of videotapes of hundreds of traffic stops in Cincinnati indicated that officers were likelier to state that they were giving the driver "a break" when the driver was not white (Ridgeway, Schell, et al., 2006). Perhaps likeliest, given some symmetry in the rates of arrest and summons, is that an officer may be likelier to arrest nonwhites rather than issue a summons. We were able to account for whether the suspect had physical or verbal identification, but the quality or validity of the identification may differ across races and would directly affect an officer's decision between arresting and issuing a summons.

Table 5.2
Comparison of Stop Outcomes for White Pedestrians with Those for Nonwhite Pedestrians Who Are Similarly Situated to the Stopped White Pedestrians

Borough	Outcome	White (%)	Black (%)	Hispanic (%)	All Nonwhite (%)
Bronx	N=	2,758	4,045	5,165	11,111
	Frisked	46.5	50.7[a]	49.8[a]	50.3[a]
	Searched	8.5	9.0	8.6	8.7
	Summon issued	7.8	7.0	7.1	6.8
	Arrested	4.9	5.2	5.1	5.1
	Force used	30.3	29.5	28.9	29.5
Brooklyn North	N=	4,705	2,391	5,099	12,772
	Frisked	24.7	27.7[a]	28.2[a]	28.4[a]
	Searched	3.0	3.4	3.5	3.6
	Summon issued	6.7	5.4[a]	5.1[a]	5.3[a]
	Arrested	1.7	1.8	1.9	2.0
	Force used	10.0	10.6	10.3	10.8
Brooklyn South	N=	13,270	2,256	3,186	4,105
	Frisked	29.0	30.9[a]	31.4[a]	30.7[a]
	Searched	5.6	6.1	5.9	5.5
	Summon issued	5.5	4.8	5.5	5.1
	Arrested	4.0	4.5	4.4	4.0
	Force used	13.6	15.3[a]	14.3	14.9[a]
Manhattan North	N=	4,859	5,304	6,042	14,334
	Frisked	29.1	32.5[a]	32.2[a]	32.1[a]
	Searched	7.2	7.2	6.9	6.9
	Summon issued	7.0	5.8[a]	6.5	6.2[a]
	Arrested	5.2	5.8	5.0	5.2
	Force used	14.2	16.2[a]	14.9	15.6[a]
Manhattan South	N=	5,547	4,072	3,641	9,781
	Frisked	29.0	33.7[a]	33.9[a]	33.4[a]
	Searched	9.5	9.4	10.0	9.7
	Summon issued	4.5	3.5[a]	3.4[a]	3.7[a]
	Arrested	8.1	7.7	8.4	7.8
	Force used	19.3	20.9[a]	21.5[a]	20.9[a]

Table 5.2—Continued

Borough	Outcome	White (%)	Black (%)	Hispanic (%)	All Nonwhite (%)
Queens North	N=	9,811	2,907	7,730	14,828
	Frisked	34.3	38.0[a]	37.9[a]	36.8[a]
	Searched	7.3	7.7	7.8	7.3
	Summon issued	5.3	4.6	5.8	5.5
	Arrested	5.1	5.7	6.2[a]	5.7[a]
	Force used	12.7	14.1[a]	13.5	13.1
Queens South	N=	4,074	3,635	4,282	8,544
	Frisked	31.6	36.6[a]	33.3	34.2[a]
	Searched	7.4	8.2	8.1	7.9
	Summon issued	6.5	6.2	6.9	6.6
	Arrested	6.5	6.2	5.8	6.1
	Force used	18.7	20.3	19.2	19.8
Staten Island	N=	8,476	1,069	663	1,908
	Frisked	20.3	29.2[a]	24.5[a]	26.2[a]
	Searched	4.8	8.1[a]	4.6	6.1[a]
	Summon issued	4.7	3.3[a]	4.7	4.0
	Arrested	4.0	6.9[a]	4.1	5.4[a]
	Force used	10.1	13.5[a]	12.0[a]	12.4[a]
Overall	Frisked	29.3	33.5[a]	32.8[a]	32.6[a]
	Searched	6.4	7.2[a]	6.7	6.7
	Summon issued	5.7	4.8[a]	5.5	5.2[a]
	Arrested	4.8	5.4[a]	5.1	5.1[a]
	Force used	14.5	16.2[a]	15.4[a]	15.7[a]

SOURCE: Computed from NYPD (2006).

NOTE: In this table, stops of black, Hispanic, and all nonwhite pedestrians are reweighted to have the same distribution of features as those of the stopped white pedestrians.

[a] Figures that differ statistically from the rate for black pedestrians.

Use of physical force includes hands-on physical restraint and handcuffing as well as use of force instruments, such as a baton or pepper spray, and drawing a firearm. Rates of use of force were fairly evenly distributed across the racial groups. In five boroughs, the rate of use of force was about 1.5 percent higher for black pedestrians than for white pedestrians. The race effect for use of force appears to be greatest in Staten Island, where officers used force on black suspects in 13.5 percent of stops compared with 10.1 percent for white suspects. This translates into an estimated 36 stops (3.4 percent of 1,069) of black suspects involving force in excess of what would be expected, judging by similarly situated stops of white pedestrians.

The results shown in Table 5.2 are the result of matching nonwhites to have the same distribution of features as white pedestrians. Matching in this way investigates how nonwhites fare in the times, places, and situations in which white suspects are detained. Instead, to assess whether racial disparities occur in the common contexts in which officers stop black suspects, we repeated the analysis, this time creating additional sets of matched stops specifically constructed for black suspects.

Table 5.3 shows the results of the analysis comparing black with similarly situated Hispanic, white, and the collection of nonblack pedestrians. The rates shown in Table 5.3 differ

Table 5.3
Comparison of Stop Outcomes for Black Pedestrians with Those for Pedestrians of Other Races Who Are Similarly Situated to the Stopped Black Pedestrians

Borough	Outcome	Black	Hispanic	White	Nonblack
Bronx	N=	36,165	20,376	724	26,916
	Frisked	57.2	55.9[a]	53.3[a]	55.2[a]
	Searched	9.4	8.7[a]	9.7	8.7[a]
	Summon issued	8.1	8.6[a]	8.8	8.6[a]
	Arrested	5.3	5.0	5.2	5.0
	Force used	27.0	26.1[a]	26.9	26.3[a]
Brooklyn North	N=	79,950	9,123	1,451	13,014
	Frisked	39.3	38.1[a]	34.1[a]	37.7[a]
	Searched	3.5	3.2	2.8	3.2
	Summon issued	5.4	5.2	6.1	5.2
	Arrested	1.8	1.4[a]	1.4	1.4[a]
	Force used	12.3	12.0	11.2	12.0
Brooklyn South	N=	32,887	1,777	567	3,086
	Frisked	55.1	53.7	53.7	54.2
	Searched	7.2	6.8	6.5	7.1
	Summon issued	3.9	4.4	5.5[a]	4.8[a]
	Arrested	3.6	3.7	3.8	3.9
	Force used	28.6	29.9	22.1[a]	28.6
Manhattan North	N=	44,964	9,256	1,326	13,655
	Frisked	46.4	45.5	44.3	44.7[a]
	Searched	7.5	7.5	7.1	7.5
	Summon issued	6.5	6.9	7.7	7.0
	Arrested	4.4	4.0	4.5	4.0[a]
	Force used	23.2	22.1[a]	22.0	21.5[a]

Table 5.3—Continued

Borough	Outcome	Black	Hispanic	White	Nonblack
Manhattan South	N=	17,915	6,345	2,441	11,230
	Frisked	37.1	37.7	32.0[a]	35.7[a]
	Searched	8.8	8.9	8.5	8.5
	Summon issued	2.4	2.3	2.6	2.4
	Arrested	6.4	6.3	7.0	6.2
	Force used	20.1	20.4	18.9	19.5
Queens North	N=	9,578	2,670	559	3,050
	Frisked	35.6	36.9	31.9[a]	35.3
	Searched	8.3	8.5	6.2[a]	8.0
	Summon issued	10.2	10.1	8.6	9.7
	Arrested	7.4	7.5	6.7	7.0
	Force used	13.5	13.0	12.0	12.5[a]
Queens South	N=	39,265	3,346	509	3,995
	Frisked	45.9	43.2[a]	44.9	43.3[a]
	Searched	7.2	7.4	9.3	7.1
	Summon issued	5.7	6.8[a]	7.7[a]	6.6[a]
	Arrested	4.9	4.1[a]	7.1[a]	4.4
	Force used	28.1	25.3[a]	31.8	26.6[a]
Staten Island	N=	6,742	1,705	683	3,558
	Frisked	37.7	34.5[a]	33.4[a]	34.1[a]
	Searched	8.7	7.5	8.5	8.0
	Summon issued	3.3	3.3	2.8	3.2
	Arrested	7.3	6.3	8.1	6.7
	Force used	22.9	22.4	21.8	22.0
Overall	Frisked	45.5	44.3[a]	42.1[a]	43.3[a]
	Searched	6.6	6.4	6.5	6.4
	Summon issued	5.7	6.0[a]	6.7[a]	6.3[a]
	Arrested	4.0	3.7[a]	4.3	3.9
	Force used	21.3	20.6[a]	20.2[a]	20.4[a]

SOURCE: Computed from NYPD (2006).

NOTE: In this table, stops of Hispanic, white, and all nonblack (includes Hispanic and white) pedestrians are reweighted to have the same distribution of features as those of the stopped black pedestrians.

[a] Figures that differ statistically from the rate for black pedestrians.

from those shown in Table 5.2 because these stops have been reweighted to reflect the contexts (e.g., times, places, reasons) in which officers commonly stop black pedestrians. Comparisons between the columns for black and white pedestrians in Table 5.3 address the unanswered issue left from the white-nonwhite comparisons in Table 5.2: Perhaps bias occurs in the contexts in which officers detain black pedestrians. Generally, black pedestrians have a greater frequency of negative outcomes from the stops, though this pattern does not appear in all boroughs or for all outcomes. For example, black pedestrians have a frisk rate that is about 2 percent higher than that for similarly situated nonblack pedestrians. Statistically, these are not chance differences. While the percentage-point difference may seem small, black pedestrians account for 267,466 stops, implying that the 2 percent difference amounts to an excess of 5,350 black pedestrians frisked. Staten Island has the largest gaps in frisk rates, as much as 4 percent. Disparities in search rates appear to be minimal, because search rates across the racial groups are nearly equal.

There are few differences in the rates of receiving a summons for black suspects than those for similarly situated suspects of the other races. In the Bronx and Brooklyn South, the rate was slightly lower for black suspects, which may suggest that officers either are likelier to give them a break or are initiating some stops of black suspects in which the likelihood of criminal activity is minimal.

Force was slightly likelier to be used against black suspects than against similarly situated nonblack suspects. However, the UF250 does not document whether the suspect cooperated with the officers. If black suspects are likelier to flee or resist, the observed difference in rates of use of force may not be due to officer bias. The largest observed difference was in Queens South, with a 1.5 percent difference in the rate of use of force. Citywide, the rate of force being used against a black suspect was about 3.9 percent larger than it was for a similarly situated nonblack suspect and 4.9 percent larger than for a similarly situated white suspect. If black suspects experienced the use-of-force rate that nonblack suspects experienced, there would have been 2,000 fewer use-of-force incidents in stops of black pedestrians.

Analysis of Hit Rates

Chapter Two of this report suggests that the *hit rate*, the rate at which contraband has been recovered from frisked or searched suspects, might be a useful measure of racial disparities in searches. If the hit rate for searched nonwhite suspects is less than the hit rate for searched white suspects, police might be applying a lower standard of suspicion to nonwhite suspects when deciding whether to search. As with the analyses presented in previous chapters, simple comparisons of hit rates can distort the true differences. A simple example demonstrates.

Assume that suspects are stopped for either burglary or robbery. Further assume that there is no racial difference in the rates at which suspects carry contraband and that police are racially neutral in making stop and frisk decisions (essentially blind to race). Last, consider the information shown in Table 5.4. Within a crime category, hit rates are equal for black and white suspects. In this example, officers detain many more white suspects on suspicion of robbery, a crime with a higher hit rate, than they do black suspects, who are likelier to be stopped for burglary. In this example, though, those large differences in the rates of stops for burglary and robbery by race are due not to officer bias but to other factors, such as racial differences in criminal participation. As a result, the total hit rate for white suspects is 4.6 percent

Table 5.4
Hypothetical Example of a Hit-Rate Analysis

Race	Measure	Burglary	Robbery
White	Stopped and frisked	100	900
	Had contraband	1	5
	Had contraband	1	45
Black	Stopped and frisked	900	100
	Had contraband	1	5
	Had contraband	9	5

([1+45]/1,000), and, for black suspects, the hit rate is 1.4 percent ([9+5]/1,000). One could conclude from these two numbers alone that racially biased officers overfrisk black suspects and underfrisk white suspects, but officers in the example are race neutral by design. Hit rates are equal across races for suspected burglars and equal across races for suspected robbers. This is a reminder that failing to account for an important factor—suspected crime, in this example—can distort the conclusions.

This example illustrates a statistical problem that Ayres (2002) termed the *subgroup validity problem*,[1] in which a particular relevant feature is more prevalent for certain racial groups. Other factors may impact the hit rate as well. Officers in some precincts may be likelier to frisk, due to crime in the area, recent surges in weapon recoveries, or a recent shooting of a fellow officer. An elevated frisk rate in some precincts may not meet with the community's approval; however, it would be premature to attribute this variation to racial bias without examining other factors. Therefore, it is critical to account for factors that might be associated with both race and the rate of contraband recovery.

We used the same analytical framework as we did for our analysis of stop outcomes to address the question of disparities in hit rates. We used all of the variables listed in Table 5.1 along with the 20 additional variables described following Table 5.1. Table 5.5 shows the results. We focused the analysis on comparisons of black, Hispanic, and white suspects, since other nonwhite groups had too few similarly situated stops that could be included in the analysis.

Frisked or searched white suspects were likelier to have contraband of some form. Black and Hispanic suspects stopped in situations that were similar to the collection of white suspects had hit rates of 5.7 percent and 5.4 percent, respectively, compared with a hit rate of 6.4 percent for white suspects. There was no statistical evidence for a difference between the recovery rates from frisks and searches of black suspects and those for similarly situated Hispanic and white suspects. Furthermore, for all racial comparisons, there were no differences in the rates at which officers found weapons on suspects.

It is plausible that the *carry rates*, the percentage of stopped suspects that have contraband, differ by race. If white suspects simply carry drugs more frequently, perhaps believing that officers are unlikely to search them, then the contraband recovery rates for white suspects will be higher. Knowles, Persico, and Todd (2001) theorized that criminals will be able to accurately assess their risk of being searched and adjust their frequency of carrying drugs and weapons

[1] This is more generally known as Yule's reversal paradox or Simpson's paradox.

Table 5.5
Frisked or Searched Suspects Found Having Contraband or Weapons

Outcome	Reference Group (%)	Comparison Racial Groups (adjusted) (%)	
	White	Black	Hispanic
Any contraband	6.4	5.7[a]	5.4[a]
Weapon	1.2	0.9	1.1
	Black	Hispanic	White
Any contraband	3.3	3.2	3.8
Weapon	0.7	0.7	0.8

SOURCE: Computed from NYPD (2006).

NOTE: Numbers from the comparison racial groups differ from those in Table 2.1 because their stops have been reweighted to have the same distribution of features as the reference group.

[a] Figures that differ statistically from the rate for the reference group.

accordingly, so that an outcome test will be appropriate. It is difficult to confirm this in practice, and, as a result, conclusions drawn from Table 5.5 must allow for the possibility that carry rates are not uniform across racial groups.

Conclusions

The citywide aggregate figures showed large differences between racial groups in the rates of frisk, search, use of force, and arrest. Accounting for important factors, such as time, place, and reason for the stop, indicates that a large portion of that gap is actually due to differences in these factors and not necessarily race.

After adjusting for stop circumstances, we found differences in the rates of some outcomes in some boroughs. On average, nonwhites experience more intrusive stops than do similarly situated white suspects. The Staten Island borough stands out particularly, with several large racial gaps in the frisk, search, and use-of-force rates.

The aggregate figures on contraband recovery rates were, perhaps, the most startling, given that recovery rates for white suspects were nearly twice those for black suspects. However, after accounting for several important factors, the recovery rate for white suspects is 12 percent greater than that for black suspects (6.4 percent versus 5.7 percent). When considering only recovery rates of weapons, we find no differences at all by race. For every 1,000 frisks of black suspects, officers recovered seven weapons; for every 1,000 frisks of similarly situated white suspects, they recovered eight weapons, a difference that is not statistically significant.

CHAPTER SIX

Conclusions and Recommendations

Conclusions

Racial differences in SQF rates generated substantial concern in New York in the early part of 2007 and continue to be discussed in the media and by policymakers. The volume of stops is cited as a cause for a large number of complaints and lawsuits against the police. Furthermore, only 10 percent of the stops result in an arrest or a summons. The value of those arrests compared with the cost of the false positives is a topic worthy of discussion in the community. Is the value of one arrest worth the cost of nine stops of suspects who have committed no crime and are not arrested? Statistical analysis cannot provide the answer.

The racial disparities in the stops have generated as much concern as has the volume of stops; 89 percent of the stops involved nonwhites, 45 percent of black and Hispanic suspects were frisked compared with 29 percent of white suspects, and, when frisked, white suspects were 70 percent likelier than were black suspects to have had a weapon on them. Our analysis clarified these observed disparities. The racial distribution of stops was similar to the racial distribution of arrestees in most categories. Hispanics were stopped 5 to 10 percent more than their representation in crime-suspect descriptions would predict. Black suspects, on the other hand, were stopped substantially less than would be expected, 20 to 30 percent less than their representation in crime-suspect descriptions.

Officers frisked 29 percent of stopped white suspects, 34 percent of similarly situated black suspects, and 33 percent of similarly situated Hispanic suspects. Note that the latter rates are much lower than the aggregate rate of 45 percent previously mentioned. Three-fourths of the racial gap in frisk rates was due to differences in time, place, and other situational factors. There remains a difference of 4 percent that none of the numerous factors included in the analysis can explain.

Analysis of data on weapons recovered from searches and frisks revealed that weapon recovery rates were nearly equal across racial groups of similarly situated suspects. The aggregate figure that frisked white suspects were 70 percent likelier to have a weapon than was a black suspect is distorted by racial differences in time, place, and reason for the stop. Regarding all contraband, such as weapons, stolen property, or drugs, when we compared white, black, and Hispanic suspects who were matched to have similar stop features, we learned that recovery rates are nearly the same (whites have slightly higher rates), suggesting that officers apply nearly the same standard of suspicion regardless of race.

Comparing thousands of stops at a time across entire boroughs can miss some of the problems that might be occurring on a smaller scale. We assessed whether there were evidence that certain officers may be disproportionately stopping nonwhites. Our analysis flagged a total of 15 officers who appear to have been stopping nonwhites substantially more than were other officers patrolling at the same time and place and in the same assignment. This represents 0.5 percent of the NYPD officers most active in pedestrian-stop activity. Again, while we found some evidence of unequal treatment across racial groups, our analysis estimates that the problem is not of a massive scale, but rather one that police management can address with effective supervision, monitoring of police activity, and effective interventions when problems are identified.

NYPD has invested heavily in the use of information to monitor crime patterns, nimbly adapt to emerging trends, and evaluate its force allocation. Those skills, to which the crime drop in New York is at times attributed, can also be effective at monitoring for problematic officers, precinct-level disparities in frisk and recovery rates, and evaluating the effect of training and policy changes on racial disparities. Such effort communicated effectively to the community members can be constructive for improving police-community relations.

Recommendations

Overall, we have six recommendations for NYPD to improve interactions between police and pedestrians during stops and to improve the accuracy of data collected during pedestrian stops.

Officers Should Clearly Explain to Pedestrians Why They Are Being Stopped

In 90 percent of the stops, the detained individual is neither arrested nor issued a summons. To mitigate the discomfort of such interactions and to bolster community trust, officers should explain the reason for the stop, discuss specifically the suspect's manner that generated the suspicion, and offer the contact information of a supervisor or appropriate complaint authority so that the person stopped can convey any positive or negative comments about the interaction. While the latter suggestion might increase the number of official complaints, it might also reduce the number of unofficial complaints that would otherwise circulate in the suspect's social network. For a trial period in select precincts, the NYPD could require that officers give an information card to those stopped pedestrians who are neither arrested nor issued a summons. An evaluation of the program could identify the kinds of stops likeliest to result in positive or negative feedback from the stopped pedestrians. Most important, ongoing communication and negotiation with the community about SQF activities are helpful in maintaining good police-community relations.

The NYPD Should Review the Boroughs with the Largest Racial Disparities in Stop Outcomes

For most stop outcomes in most parts of the city, we found few, if any, racial differences in the rates of frisk, search, arrest, and use of force. However, for some particular subsets of stops, there are racial disparities, and, in some boroughs for some outcomes, the disparities are fairly large. In particular, there was evidence of large racial differences in frisk rates in several boroughs. For example, on Staten Island, officers frisk 20 percent of white suspects and 29 percent of similarly situated black suspects. Officers were likelier to use force of some kind against black suspects in Brooklyn South than they were to use it against similarly situated white suspects (29 percent versus 22 percent). However, the use-of-force finding on which we base this recommendation may be the result of incomplete details on the reason officers used force, the subject of the next recommendation. Regardless, a closer review of these outcomes in these boroughs may suggest changes in training, policies, or practices that can reduce these disparities.

The UF250 Should Be Revised to Capture Data on Use of Force

All of the reported differences resulting from our analysis are potentially due to unobserved or unmeasured features of the stops rather than racial bias. For example, the 1 percent difference observed in rates of use of force between stops of white and nonwhite suspects may be due to a factor not recorded on the UF250. It is possible that nonwhite suspects were slightly likelier to attempt to flee or threaten officers. If the percentage of nonwhite-pedestrian stops in which the suspect resisted officers was 0.8 percent more than the frequency with which white suspects resisted officers, statistically, the frisk rates would be indistinguishable. However, these reasons—attempting to flee or resisting officers—are not recorded on the UF250. The UF250 was intended for investigative purposes and not for assessing officer performance or racial disparities. For the data to be more useful for careful analysis of racial bias in use-of-force incidents, the reason for the use of force needs to be recorded.

New Officers Should Be Fully Conversant with Stop, Question, and Frisk Documentation Policies

Officers with more than one year of experience seemed fully informed of the SQF practices and documentation policies. However, informal discussions with and observations of recent academy graduates indicated that some were not fully aware of the documentation policies and procedures, despite a substantial investment of time in the academy training curriculum on SQF. This is an issue that likely impacts a small fraction of stops. For the purposes of assessing racial bias, we do not find a need for investment to correct this, but, since data on UF250s are used in other facets of NYPD evaluation, some correction in training during new officers' initial days on the street might be in order, particularly for any evaluation of impact programs.

The NYPD Should Consider Modifying the Audits of the UF250

The NYPD has multiple layers of auditing to ensure that the UF250s are complete and contain valid and sufficiently detailed entries to each question. This does not address whether stops are occurring that are not documented. Since officers have an incentive to demonstrate productivity through UF250s, most stops should be documented. However, particularly problematic ones may not be. Radio communications could be monitored for a fixed period in a few randomly selected precincts. Notes of the times and places of street encounters that should have associated UF250s can be noted and requests made for the forms.

All of our analyses rely on the data that officers record on UF250s. The accuracy of the information on the forms, such as time, place, and reason for the stop, is assumed to be approximately correct for the purposes of our analyses. For inaccuracies to adversely affect our analyses, officers would have had to consistently record events differently for nonwhite than for white suspects. However, unless officers were carefully tabulating which actions they failed to report, the analyses in this report would interpret the patterns that would result as evidence of a disparity. For example, if officers consistently did not record frisks of nonwhite suspects, our analysis would have found white suspects to be substantially overfrisked. There is no evidence of such general patterns. That said, in interpreting the findings of this study, we must offer the caveat that systematic misreporting of data on the UF250 could potentially distort the findings.

NYPD Should Identify, Flag, and Investigate Officers with Out-of-the-Ordinary Stop Patterns

Our analysis indicates that the racial distribution of stops for several officers is skewed substantially from those of their colleagues. We recommend that the NYPD review these flagged officers and incorporate into their early warning system a component that flags officers with extreme deviations from their colleagues. These measured disparities are evidence that these officers differ substantially from their peers; however, they are not necessarily conclusive evidence that these officers practice racially biased policing. Supervisors may then investigate and address the disparities.

APPENDIX A

Details of Statistical Models Used in the External-Benchmark Analysis

Statistical Model for Comparisons with the Residential Census

Let y_{ij} indicate the number of stops of suspects in precinct i who are of race j, and let n_i be the total number of stops in precinct i. Let p_{ij} indicate the percentage of residents in precinct i who are members of race j. We modeled the counts of stops as a Poisson and allowed for the rate to vary by precinct and by race: $y_{ij} \sim \text{Poisson}(p_{ij} n_i \alpha_j)$.

The term $p_{ij} n_i$ essentially represents the expected number of stopped suspects of race j if the stop pattern reflected the residential census. The primary term of interest is α_j, a multiplier that depends on race that either increases or decreases the expected number of stopped suspects, depending on their race. This model can be fit with standard software for generalized linear models, restricting there to be no intercept, an offset term of $\log\left(p_{ij} n_i\right)$, and a categorical race effect.

There is a well-known connection between the Poisson distribution and the multinomial. If $(y_{i1}, y_{i2}, y_{i3}, y_{i4}, y_{i5})$ are the counts in precinct i, then $(y_{i1}, y_{i2}, y_{i3}, y_{i4}, y_{i5})$ conditional on their sum being equal to n_i has a multinomial distribution with probabilities $(p_{i1}\alpha_j/K_i, p_{i2}\alpha_j/K_i, p_{i3}\alpha_j/K_i, p_{i4}\alpha_j/K_i, p_{i5}\alpha_j/K_i)$, where K_i is the normalizing constant that makes the terms sum to 1.

Statistical Model for Comparisons with 2005 Arrestees

Let y_{ij} indicate the number of stops of suspects in precinct i who are of race j, and let n_{ij} be the number of arrestees from precinct i who are of race j. We used a variation on the statistical model proposed in Gelman, Fagan, and Kiss (2007, equation 4):

$$y_{ij} \sim \text{Poisson}(\theta_{ij}\exp[\mu + \beta_i + \alpha_j + \varepsilon_{ij})$$

$$n_{ij} \sim \text{Poisson}(\theta_{ij}).$$

We constrained the sum of the β_is and the sum of the α_js to equal 0. The term $\theta_{ij}\exp(\mu + \beta_i)$ captures the expected number of stops of suspects of race j in precinct i. The multiplier $\exp(\alpha_j)$ indicates whether the rate of stops of race j appears to be in excess of what would be expected. The term ε_{ij} is modeled as a $\text{Normal}\left(0, \sigma^2\right)$ random variable, to allow for extra-Poisson variability (overdispersion) in the outcome.

Gelman, Fagan, and Kiss (2007) attempted to further decompose θ_{ij} into components representing the residential census, race, and precinct, but that additional structure is not necessary for the estimation of the race effect, $\exp(\alpha_j)$.

We estimated the parameters using OpenBUGS 3.0.1.

APPENDIX B

Details of Propensity-Score Weighting

We used propensity-score weighting to reweight stops from some comparison groups to have the same distribution of features as the stops in a reference group. The choice of reference and comparison groups differs by the analytical question being addressed. In Chapter Four, stops from one officer formed the reference group, and the collection of other officers' stops comprised the comparison group. In Chapter Five, stops involving suspects of one racial group formed the reference group, and stops of suspects of other races comprised the comparison group.

Stops in the comparison are weighted and are not technically included or excluded from the sample. The weights are constructed in such a way that any weighted statistic of the comparison group (e.g., weighted average age, weighted percentage from precinct 14, weighted percentage stopped between midnight and 4 a.m. resulting from a radio run) will match the same unweighted statistic computed for the reference group.

Let $\mathbf{x}$ represent the collection of stop features and t be a binary indicator that the stop is a member of the reference group. The distribution $f(\mathbf{x}|t=1)$ represents the conditional distribution of stop features for those stops in the reference group, and $f(\mathbf{x}|t=0)$ represents the distribution of features for stops in the comparison group. We wanted to weight the latter distribution so that

$$f(\mathbf{x}|t=1) = w(\mathbf{x})\, f(\mathbf{x}|t=0),$$

where $w(\mathbf{x})$ is the weighting function of interest to us. Solving for $w(\mathbf{x})$ and applying Bayes' theorem to the numerator and denominator yields

$$w(\mathbf{x}) = K f(t=1|\mathbf{x}) / f(t=0|\mathbf{x}),$$

where K is a constant that will later drop out of the analysis. The right-side expression is proportional to the probability that a stop with features $\mathbf{x}$ is in the reference group divided by the probability that a stop with features $\mathbf{x}$ is in the comparison group.

This indicates that, for a comparison-group stop with features $\mathbf{x}$, we should apply a weight equal to the odds that a stop with features $\mathbf{x}$ was in the reference group. Note that, if reference-group stops rarely occur in precinct 14, for example, then all comparison-group stops made in precinct 14 will receive a weight near 0. On the other hand, comparison-group stops with features much like those of the reference group will receive large weights.

To estimate $f(t=1|\mathbf{x})$, we used a nonparametric version of logistic regression. See McCaffrey, Ridgeway, and Morral (2004) for complete details. We evaluated the quality of the weights by how well the distribution of the features matched between the reference group and the weighted stops in the comparison group. For example, comparing the third and fourth columns in Table 4.1 in Chapter Four indicates that the computed weights align the distribution of stop features for nonwhite suspects with the distribution of stop features for white suspects.

APPENDIX C

Estimating False Discovery Rates

Fridell (2004) noted that a popular statistic for measuring the difference between an officer's nonwhite-pedestrian stop fraction and the officer's internal benchmark is the z-statistic,

$$z = \frac{p_t - p_c}{\sqrt{\frac{p_t(1-p_t)}{N_t} + \frac{p_c(1-p_c)}{N_c}}}. \qquad \text{C.1}$$

In this measure, p_t and p_c are, respectively, the proportion of stops involving nonwhite pedestrians for the target and the weighted comparison-group stops. The denominator normalizes this term to have variance 1. This statistic is computed for all officers under consideration. In standard circumstances, z will have a standard normal distribution, and the probability that the absolute value of z exceeds 2.0 when there is no difference between the officer's stop rate and the internal benchmark is 5 percent. However, in a collection of 2,756 *independent* comparisons with no racial bias, we should expect about 138 (5 percent of 2,756) officers to have z-statistics exceeding 2.0 by chance. Thus, flagging officers with z exceeding 2.0 is bound to select officers with no racial biases. Further complicating matters is that the 2,756 z-scores are *not* independent. They are correlated with each other, since each officer might be used in another officer's internal benchmark. In this case, the empirical distribution of the zs may be much wider (or narrower) than would be predicted by statistical theory (Efron, 2006).

Benjamini and Hochberg (1995) pioneered the use of the false discovery rate (fdr) as an alternative methodology for locating truly extreme values in multiple comparison situations. The fdr is the probability of no group difference given the value of an observed test statistic, z (Efron, 2004).

We can derive the probability of an officer being outlier as

$$\begin{aligned} P(\text{outlier} \mid z) &= 1 - P(\text{not outlier} \mid z) \\ &= 1 - \frac{f(z \mid \text{not outlier}) f(\text{not outlier})}{f(z)} \\ &\geq 1 - \frac{f_0(z)}{f(z)}, \end{aligned} \qquad \text{C.2}$$

where $f_0(z)$ is the distribution of z for nonoutlier officers, and $f(z)$ is the distribution of z for all officers (Efron, 2004). If the fraction of problem officers is small (less than 10 percent), the bound in the last line of Equation C.2 is near equality. We estimated $f_0(z)$ with the empirical null assuming normal but with location and variance estimated using only the central data of the distribution.

We used the R package locfdr 1.1-4 for this analysis' calculations.

APPENDIX D

Unified Form 250: Stop, Question, and Frisk Report Worksheet

The following pages contain a copy of the UF250.

(COMPLETE ALL CAPTIONS)

STOP, QUESTION AND FRISK REPORT WORKSHEET
PD344-151A (Rev. 11-02)

Pct.Serial No.	
Date	Pct. Of Occ.

Time Of Stop	Period Of Observation Prior To Stop	Radio Run/Sprint #

Address/Intersection Or Cross Streets Of Stop

☐ Inside ☐ Outside	☐ Transit ☐ Housing	Type Of Location Describe:

Specify Which Felony/P.L. Misdemeanor Suspected	Duration Of Stop

What Were Circumstances Which Led To Stop?
(MUST CHECK AT LEAST ONE BOX)

- ☐ Carrying Objects In Plain View Used In Commission Of Crime e.g., Slim Jim/Pry Bar, etc.
- ☐ Fits Description.
- ☐ Actions Indicative Of "Casing" Victim Or Location.
- ☐ Actions Indicative of Acting As A Lookout.
- ☐ Suspicious Bulge/Object (Describe)
- ☐ Other Reasonable Suspicion Of Criminal Activity (Specify)
- ☐ Actions Indicative Of Engaging In Drug Transaction.
- ☐ Furtive Movements.
- ☐ Actions Indicative Of Engaging In Violent Crimes.
- ☐ Wearing Clothes/Disguises Commonly Used In Commission Of Crime.

Name Of Person Stopped	Nickname/ Street Name	Date Of Birth

Address	Apt. No.	Tel. No.

Identification: ☐ Verbal ☐ Photo I.D. ☐ Refused
☐ Other (Specify) ____________________

Sex: ☐ Male ☐ Female	Race: ☐ White ☐ Black ☐ White Hispanic ☐ Black Hispanic ☐ Asian/Pacific Islander ☐ American Indian/Alaskan Native

Age	Height	Weight	Hair	Eyes	Build

Other (Scars, Tattoos, Etc.)

Did Officer Explain Reason For Stop ☐ Yes ☐ No	If No, Explain:

Were Other Persons Stopped/ Questioned/Frisked? ☐ Yes ☐ No	If Yes, List Pct. Serial Nos.

If Physical Force Was Used, Indicate Type:

- ☐ Hands On Suspect
- ☐ Suspect On Ground
- ☐ Pointing Firearm At Suspect
- ☐ Handcuffing Suspect
- ☐ Suspect Against Wall/Car
- ☐ Drawing Firearm
- ☐ Baton
- ☐ Pepper Spray
- ☐ Other (Describe)

Was Suspect Arrested? ☐ Yes ☐ No	Offense	Arrest No.
Was Summons Issued? ☐ Yes ☐ No	Offense	Summons No.
Officer In Uniform? ☐ Yes ☐ No	If No, How Identified? ☐ Shield ☐ I.D. Card ☐ Verbal	

Was Person Frisked? ☐ Yes ☐ No **IF YES, MUST CHECK AT LEAST ONE BOX**

- ☐ Inappropriate Attire - Possibly Concealing Weapon
- ☐ Verbal Threats Of Violence By Suspect
- ☐ Knowledge Of Suspects Prior Criminal Violent Behavior/Use Of Force/Use Of Weapon
- ☐ Other Reasonable Suspicion of Weapons (Specify)
- ☐ Furtive Movements
- ☐ Actions Indicative Of Engaging In Violent Crimes
- ☐ Refusal To Comply With Officer's Direction(s) Leading To Reasonable Fear For Safety
- ☐ Violent Crime Suspected
- ☐ Suspicious Bulge/Object (Describe)

Was Person Searched? ☐ Yes ☐ No **IF YES, MUST CHECK AT LEAST ONE BOX** ☐ Hard Object ☐ Admission Of Weapons Possession
☐ Outline Of Weapon ☐ Other Reasonable Suspicion of Weapons (Specify)

Was Weapon Found? ☐ Yes ☐ No If Yes, Describe: ☐ Pistol/Revolver ☐ Rifle/Shotgun ☐ Assault Weapon ☐ Knife/Cutting Instrument
☐ Machine Gun ☐ Other (Describe)

Was Other Contraband Found? ☐ Yes ☐ No If Yes, Describe Contraband And Location ____________________
Demeanor Of Person After Being Stopped ____________________
Remarks Made By Person Stopped

Additional Circumstances/Factors: (Check All That Apply)

- ☐ Report From Victim/Witness
- ☐ Area Has High Incidence Of Reported Offense Of Type Under Investigation
- ☐ Time Of Day, Day Of Week, Season Corresponding To Reports Of Criminal Activity
- ☐ Suspect Is Associating With Persons Known For Their Criminal Activity
- ☐ Proximity To Crime Location
- ☐ Other (Describe)
- ☐ Evasive, False Or Inconsistent Response To Officer's Questions
- ☐ Changing Direction At Sight Of Officer/Flight
- ☐ Ongoing Investigations, e.g., Robbery Pattern
- ☐ Sights And Sounds Of Criminal Activity, e.g., Bloodstains, Ringing Alarms

Pct. Serial No. ______ | Additional Reports Prepared: Complaint Rpt.No. ______ Juvenile Rpt. No. ______ Aided Rpt. No. ______ Other Rpt. (Specify) _____

REPORTED BY: Rank, Name (Last, First, M.I.)		REVIEWED BY: Rank, Name (Last, First, M.I.)	
Print ____________________	Tax# __________	Print ____________________	Tax# __________
Signature ____________________	Command __________	Signature ____________________	Command _______

References

Ayres, Ian, "Outcome Tests of Racial Disparities in Police Practices," *Justice Research and Policy*, Vol. 4, No. 1, 2002, pp. 131–142.

Benjamini, Yoav, and Yosef Hochberg, "Controlling the False Discovery Rate: A Practical and Powerful Approach to Multiple Testing," *Journal of the Royal Statistical Society, Series B (Methodological)*, Vol. 57, No. 1, 1995, pp. 289–300.

BJS—*see* Bureau of Justice Statistics.

Blank, Rebecca M., Marilyn Dabady, and Constance F. Citro, eds., *Measuring Racial Discrimination*, Washington, D.C.: National Academies Press, 2004.

Bureau of Justice Statistics, "Crime Trends," last revised December 13, 2006. As of November 9, 2007: http://bjsdata.ojp.usdoj.gov/dataonline/Search/Crime/Crime.cfm

———, *Census of State and Local Law Enforcement Agencies*, Washington, D.C.: U.S. Dept. of Justice, Office of Justice Programs, Bureau of Justice Statistics, June 2007. As of November 9, 2007: http://www.ojp.usdoj.gov/bjs/abstract/csllea04.htm

Decker, Scott H., and Jeff Rojek, *Saint Louis Metropolitan Police Department Traffic Stop Patterns*, St. Louis, Mo.: University of Missouri, 2002.

Durose, Matthew R., Erica Leah Smith, and Patrick A. Langan, *Contacts Between Police and the Public: Findings from the 2002 National Survey*, Washington, D.C.: U.S. Department of Justice, Office of Justice Programs, Bureau of Justice Statistics, NCJ 207845, 2005. As of November 9, 2007: http://purl.access.gpo.gov/GPO/LPS13168

Efron, Bradley, "Large-Scale Simultaneous Hypothesis Testing: The Choice of a Null Hypothesis," *Journal of the American Statistical Association*, Vol. 99, No. 465, 2004, pp. 96–104.

———, *Correlation and Large-Scale Simultaneous Significance Testing*, 2006. As of November 9, 2007: http://www-stat.stanford.edu/~brad/papers/Correlation-2006.pdf

Fridell, Lorie A., *By the Numbers: A Guide for Analyzing Race Data from Vehicle Stops*, Washington, D.C.: Police Executive Research Forum, 2004. As of November 9, 2007: http://www.policeforum.org/upload/BytheNumbers%5B1%5D_715866088_12302005121341.pdf

Gelman, Andrew, Jeffrey Fagan, and Alex Kiss, "An Analysis of the New York City Police Department's 'Stop-and-Frisk' Policy in the Context of Claims of Racial Bias," *Journal of the American Statistical Association*, Vol. 102, No. 479, 2007, pp. 813–823.

Goode, Erich, "Drug Arrests at the Millennium," *Society*, Vol. 39, No. 5, 2002, pp. 41–45.

Grogger, Jeffrey, and Greg Ridgeway, *Testing for Racial Profiling in Traffic Stops From Behind a Veil of Darkness*, Santa Monica, Calif.: RAND Corporation, RP-1253, 2006. As of November 8, 2007: http://www.rand.org/pubs/reprints/RP1253/

Hamermesh, Daniel S., *Workdays, Workhours, and Work Schedules: Evidence for the United States and Germany*, Kalamazoo, Mich.: W. E. Upjohn Institute for Employment Research, 1996.

Kang, Joseph D. Y., and Joseph L. Schafer, "Demystifying Double Robustness: A Comparison of Alternative Strategies for Estimating a Population Mean from Incomplete Data," *Statistical Science*, submitted. As of November 9, 2007:
http://www.e-publications.org/ims/submission/index.php/STS/user/submissionFile/290?confirm=14e47e26

Klein, Stephen P., Richard A. Berk, and Laura J. Hickman, *Race and the Decision to Seek the Death Penalty in Federal Cases*, Santa Monica, Calif.: RAND Corporation, TR-389-NIJ, 2006. As of November 8, 2007:
http://www.rand.org/pubs/technical_reports/TR389/

Knowles, John, Nicola Persico, and Petra Todd, "Racial Bias in Motor Vehicle Searches: Theory and Evidence," *Journal of Political Economy*, Vol. 109, No. 1, February 2001, pp. 203–229.

McCaffrey, Daniel F., Greg Ridgeway, and Andrew R. Morral, *Propensity Score Estimation with Boosted Regression for Evaluating Causal Effects in Observational Studies*, Santa Monica, Calif.: RAND Corporation, RP-1164, 2004. As of November 9, 2007:
http://www.rand.org/pubs/reprints/RP1164/

National Institutes of Health, Office of Human Subjects Research, Federalwide Assurance for the Protection of Human Subjects: RAND Corporation, expires October 3, 2010.

National Survey on Drug Use and Health, and Substance Abuse and Mental Health Services Administration, Office of Applied Studies, *The NSDUH Report: Illicit Drug Use by Race/Ethnicity, in Metropolitan and Non-Metropolitan Counties: 2004 and 2005*, Rockville, Md.: U.S. Department of Health and Human Services, Substance Abuse and Mental Health Services Administration, Office of Applied Studies, June 19, 2007. As of November 9, 2007:
http://www.oas.samhsa.gov/2k7/popDensity/popDensity.cfm

New York City Police Department, "Street Encounters—Legal Issues," brochure, PD344-153 (11-00)-RMU, November 2000.

———, "Unified Form 250: Stop, Question, and Frisk Report Worksheet," PD344-151A, November 2002.

———, *Stop Question and Frisk Report (UF250) Database*, data for 2006, extracted March 2007.

NIH—*see* National Institutes of Health.

NYPD—*see* New York City Police Department.

Office of Justice Programs, *Justice Expenditure and Employment in the United States*, Washington, D.C.: U.S. Department of Justice, Office of Justice Programs, April 2006. As of November 9, 2007:
http://www.ojp.usdoj.gov/bjs/abstract/jeeus03.htm

People v. De Bour, 40 N.Y.2d 210, 352 N.E.2d 562, App. N.Y., June 15, 1976.

Raymond, Barbara, Laura J. Hickman, Laura Miller, and Jennifer S. Wong, *Police Personnel Challenges After September 11: Anticipating Expanded Duties and a Changing Labor Pool*, Santa Monica, Calif.: RAND Corporation, OP-154-RC, 2005. As of November 8, 2007:
http://www.rand.org/pubs/occasional_papers/OP154/

Ridgeway, Greg, *Assessing the Effect of Race Bias in Post-Traffic Stop Outcomes Using Propensity Scores*, Santa Monica, Calif.: RAND Corporation, RP-1252, 2006. As of November 9, 2007:
http://www.rand.org/pubs/reprints/RP1252/

Ridgeway, Greg, and K. Jack Riley, *Assessing Racial Profiling More Credibly*, Santa Monica, Calif.: RAND Corporation, RB-9070-OAK, 2004. As of November 8, 2007:
http://www.rand.org/pubs/research_briefs/RB9070/

Ridgeway, Greg, Terry Schell, K. Jack Riley, Susan Turner, and Travis L. Dixon, *Police-Community Relations in Cincinnati: Year Two Evaluation Report*, Santa Monica, Calif.: RAND Corporation, TR-445-CC, 2006. As of November 8, 2007:
http://www.rand.org/pubs/technical_reports/TR445/

Riley, K. Jack, Susan Turner, John MacDonald, Greg Ridgeway, Terry Schell, Jeremy M. Wilson, Travis L. Dixon, Terry Fain, Dionne Barnes-Proby, and Brent D. Fulton, *Police-Community Relations in Cincinnati*, Santa Monica, Calif.: RAND Corporation, TR-333-CC, 2005. As of November 8, 2007:
http://www.rand.org/pubs/technical_reports/TR333/

Spitzer, Eliot, *The New York City Police Department's Stop and Frisk Practices: A Report to the People of the State of New York from the Office of the Attorney General*, New York: Civil Rights Bureau, December 1, 1999. As of November 9, 2007:
http://purl.org/net/nysl/nysdocs/43037966

Terry v. Ohio, 392 U.S. 1, 88 S. Ct. 1868, June 10, 1968.

U.S. Census Bureau, *The American Community Survey*, Washington, D.C., last modified November 1, 2007. As of November 9, 2007:
http://www.census.gov/acs/www/

———, Population Division, Journey to Work and Migration Statistics Branch, "Estimated Daytime Population," last modified February 23, 2007. As of September 20, 2007:
http://www.census.gov/population/www/socdemo/daytime/daytimepop.html

United States v. Alcaraz-Arellano, 302 F. Supp. 2d 1217, D. Kan., January 22, 2004.

United States v. Barlow, 310 F.3d 1007, 7th Cir., November 18, 2002.

Walker, Samuel, "Searching for the Denominator: Problems with Police Traffic Stop Data and an Early Warning System Solution," *Justice Research and Policy*, Vol. 3, No. 2, 2001, pp. 63–95.

———, *The Citizen's Guide to Interpreting Traffic Stop Data: Unraveling the Racial Profiling Controversy*, unpublished manuscript, 2002.

———, *Internal Benchmarking for Traffic Stop Data: An Early Intervention System Approach*, 2003.